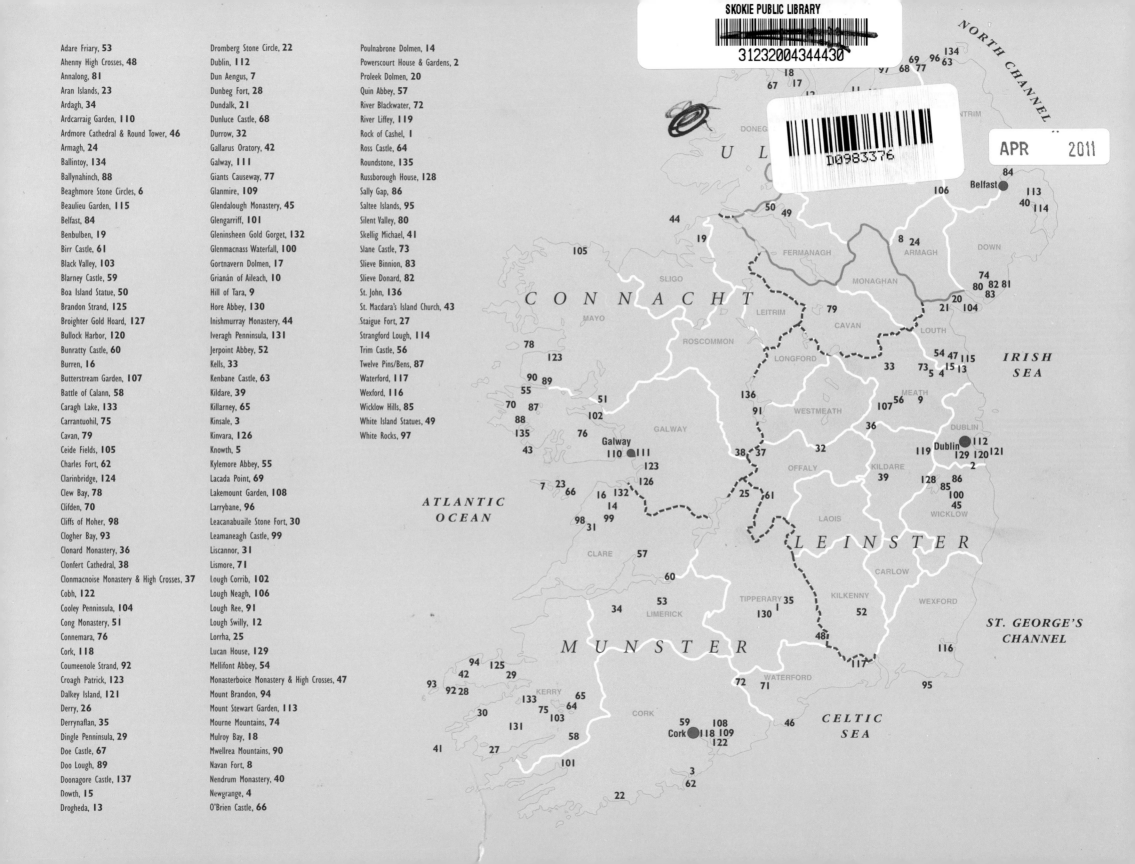

SPECTACULAR
IRELAND

Text by
Peter Harbison

Photography by

Liam Blake

Michael Diggin

Colman Doyle

Christopher Hill

Jill Jennings

Brian Lynch

George Munday

Jacqueline O'Brien

Peter Zoeller

and others

UNIVERSE

Published by
Universe Publishing,
A Division of Rizzoli International Publications, Inc.
300 Park Avenue South
New York, NY 10010
www.rizzoliusa.com

Editor and Photo Researcher: LESLIE C. CAROLA
Copy Editor: DEBORAH T. ZINDELL
Designer: DANA LEVY, Perpetua Press

Acknowledgments:
The publisher gratefully acknowledges the assistance of The Irish Tourist Board, especially Ruth Moran, Clive Brooks, and Brian Lynch; The Northern Irish Tourist Board; The Merrion Hotel, Dublin; Valerie Dowling, The National Museum of Ireland; Tony Roche, Dúchas, The Heritage Service, Dublin; Letitia Pollard, Ireland of the Welcomes, Dublin; Lady Mairi Bury, J. P., Brian Cross, Helen Dillon, Lorna Mac Mahon, and Jim Reynolds for help ,with their respective gardens; GE Munday, J J Blandford, Carrie Fonseca, Erin Parsons, and Leona McEvoy, The Slide File, Dublin; Lara Lynn Lane, Hugh Lauter Levin Associates, Inc.

Photo credits:
LIAM BLAKE (Slide File): Pages 2-3, 4-5, 6-7, 8-9, 23, 24 (bottom), 26-27, 32 (bottom), 36 (bottom), 37, 38 (left), 46 (above), 62, 66-67, 69, 71, 72-74, 76-77, 78-79, 82 (bottom), 84-85, 87 (right), 88-89, 90 (below), 94-96, 98 (top, left), 122, 124, 126, 127.
JAMIE BLANDFORD (Slide File): Pages 14, 68, 86, 87 (above), 92.
MICHAEL CORRIGAN (Slide File): Page 99.
MICHAEL DIGGIN: Pages 1, 52, 61 (left), 70, 75, 83, 91, 97, 105 (right), 136.
BILL DOYLE (Slide File): Page 98 (bottom).
COLMAN DOYLE: Pages 128, 129 (left column and middle), 130 (above, right), 131 (top row, middle row).
VALERIE DOWLING (National Museum of Ireland): Pages 17, 18 (bottom, right), 19 (left).
DÚCHAS, The Heritage Service, Dublin: Pages 22, 35, 36 (top), 38 (right).
TIM HANNEN (Slide File): Page 50 (left).
CHRISTOPHER HILL (Christopher Hill Photographic): Pages 10-12, 29, 46 (right), 54, 64, 80, 81, 82 (top), 90 (right), 93, 101, 104, 124 (left), 125, 131 (bottom).
CHRISTOPHER HILL (Slide File): Page 50 (below).
THE IRISH PICTURE LIBRARY: Pages 24 (top), 123 (all, top).
THE IRISH TOURIST BOARD: Pages 20 (Brian Lynch), 33 (Brian Lynch), 40 (right) (Brian Lynch), 121, 129 (right), 130 (left and far right).
JILL JENNINGS (Christopher Hill Photographic): Pages 16, 100 (right), 102-103, 105 (left).
THE MERRION HOTEL: Page 123 (bottom, center and right).
GEORGE MUNDAY (Slide File): Pages 32 (top), 65, 106, 107, 108, 109, 110, 111, 112, 113, 114, 115, 116, 117, 118, 119.
THE NATIONAL MUSEUM OF IRELAND: Page 18 (top, right).
THE NORTHERN IRISH TOURIST BOARD: Page 124 (right).
NUTAN (Slide File): Pages 132-134, 135.
JACQUELINE O'BRIEN: Pages 19 (top, left and right), 21, 25, 28, 30, 31, 34, 39, 40 (left), 41, 42, 44, 45, 47, 48, 49, 53, 56, 57, 58, 59, 60, 61 (right), 63, 120.
TRINITY COLLEGE, DUBLIN: Page 18 (above).
FELIX ZASKA (Slide File): Page 43 (right).
PETER ZOELLER (Slide File): Pages 43 (left), 51, 55, 98 (top, right), 100 (left), 130 (bottom, right).

Photos: Page 1: Haystacks above Caragh Lake, Co. Kerry; Pages 2-3: Hore Abbey, Rock of Cashel, Co. Tipperary; Pages 4-5: Traditional cottage near Clifden, Connemara, Co. Galway; Pages 6-7: Powerscourt Gardens, Co. Wicklow; Pages 8-9: Kinsale, Co. Cork; Pages 10-12: Ballintoy, Co. Antrim: Page 14: Twelve Bens from the bog road at Roundstone, Co. Galway.

2009 2010 2011 2012 / 10 9 8 7 6 5 4 3 2 1

Printed in China

ISBN-13: 978-0-7893-9967-0

Library of Congress Catalog Control Number: 2008933177

CONTENTS

INTRODUCTION

LOOKING BACK AT A COUNTRY'S PAST IS like peering into a telescope at the wrong end—instead of the detail getting magnified, it just seems to get smaller as it recedes. The human story of Ireland is no different from that in any other country in that the farther back we seek our roots in time, the more dwarfish our understanding of the country's earliest inhabitants becomes. This is not an effort to suggest how the leprechaun came into being, but to point out that we know so little about the people who lived in Ireland for much of the first half of the ten thousand years that humans have occupied the island. Hardy folk they must certainly have been, pitting their wits against nature, exploring up slow-flowing rivers to find fish, and penetrating the primeval forest in search of whatever protein they could discover among the dense scrub that had established itself after the glaciers had finally retreated by around 20,000 to 15,000 years ago. The necessity to still their hunger on the move meant that they had little time to stop and leave

permanent visible reminders of their presence on the Irish landscape.

It was only after a new farming community had come to settle in Ireland, and had become affluent enough to build large stone tombs a little over five thousand years ago, that the time was ripe and the talent available to initiate craftworking in Ireland, a tradition of quality that—despite many intermediate interruptions—remains active down to our own day. The earliest manifestation of that craftsmanship survives largely in stone, in the carving associated with passage tombs like Newgrange and Knowth. But the spirals, lozenges, zigzags, and other motifs that were chiselled into the stone were designs that the stonemasons probably copied from other media that have not withstood the test of time—including wood and leather, and perhaps weavings, too, which may have been hung on the walls of the houses of the living, to be copied subsequently in stone for the houses of the dead. It is a tribute to these nameless early craftspeople that they emerged at roughly the same time as the rise of one of the world's first great civilizations in pharaonic Egypt around 3000 B.C., thus making Ireland into one of Europe's earliest craft-oriented countries. These anonymous men and women laid the foundations for a love of geometrical design (in preference to naturalistic representations of the human form) that was to be characteristic of Irish art for millennia to come. During the Bronze Age (c. 2000–500 B.C.), the considerable amounts of gold that became available provided surfaces the goldsmiths could decorate with linear ornament such as hatched triangles, zigzags, and concentric circles. At the start of the period, however, the gold was still scarce and wafer-thin, providing a challenge to the metalsmith not to incise his lines too deeply, but later—in the last pre-Christian millennium—the gold became much more abundant and he could vary his techniques, which he did to great effect. In

fact, some of the workmanship of the time is so complicated and on such a minute scale that modern jewelers would find it extremely difficult to imitate it.

This gold must have made Late Bronze Age Ireland into some kind of El Dorado, and the holdings of prehistoric gold in the National Museum in Dublin have few if any equals in the whole of western Europe. But the bubble had to burst, and by the time Celtic craftsmen came along around 300 B.C. to decorate metal and stone objects in the lively curvilinear La Tène style of the continental Celts, the gold panned from Irish rivers had been almost entirely exhausted. Nevertheless, there was enough to allow them to create masterpieces such as the torque (or neck-ring) found at Broighter in Co. Derry along with a beautiful model boat of gold with oars and a mast, deposited close to the shore possibly as a votive offering to the Celtic

sea-god Manannán Mac Lir and which, with a date of around the last century before Christ, is the earliest surviving evidence for the use of sail in Irish or British waters.

Boats must have been important for this island community over the last five thousand years as bearers of people with new artistic ideas—and it is noticeable that the excellence of Irish craftsmanship is usually attested when the country was in close contact with other areas along the Atlantic coast of Europe. The Roman Empire in Britain during the first four centuries of our era had a fleet of ships, which must have made it difficult for the Irish to retain that contact, but it was in a boat that St. Patrick was brought as a captive slave from Roman Britain to Ireland in the fifth century. At the same time, Christianity was bringing a whole new stimulus across the Irish Sea in the form of literacy and the books that went with it.

The monasteries that sprang up all around the country within a hundred years of St. Patrick's death reaped the benefits of these new ideas, and set the country off on a whole new phase of the greatest artistic activity. From the sixth to the twelfth century, these monasteries became not only the fosterers of Latin learning and literature, but also the promoters of craftsmanship in a variety of media and, at the height of its brilliance in the eighth century, unmatched anywhere else in Europe. To judge by the material that survives, it started around 600 with metalwork that had somehow managed to keep alive and give new meaning to the old curving Celtic patterns of the prehistoric period. These designs were joined in due time by interlace and animal ornament, all of which taken together were to become the staple assemblage of motifs combined and modified in myriad variations in Irish art of the Golden Age. They were to be grouped together with supreme mastery in the *Book of*

Kells around 800, but a century earlier they had already played an important role in the *Book of Durrow*—both manuscripts now preserved and displayed in the Library of Trinity College, Dublin. In its evangelist symbols, such as the Eagle, the *Book of Durrow* shows the influence of metal and enamel motifs, and we must presume that the scriptorium for manuscripts must have been located sufficiently close to the metalsmith's workshop that the two could borrow mutually from one another.

Because of the nature of its material, metalwork has probably managed to survive time and destruction more than manuscripts, and the Treasury of the National Museum of Ireland in Dublin is full of wonderful metalwork, much of it, such as the St. John's Crucifixion plaque, used in the service of the church and testifying to the artistic genius of the ancient Irish monasteries.

The chalice found at Ardagh in Co. Limerick in 1868 is among the finest, combining silver, gold filigree, enamel, and glass with a taste that is exuberant without being showy. One feature of these great works of art of the period around the eighth century is the miniscule scale of the designs which, even when magnified a number of times, can be seen to be perfect in execution.

The arrival of the Vikings in the ninth century must undoubtedly have had a debilitating and unsettling effect on monastic production, and they are likely to have been responsible, at least in part, for the decline in metalwork and manuscripts after 800. But, equally, their carrying off of monastic metalwork to their Scandinavian homeland may have been a contributing factor in the creation of those less easily movable and certainly monumental stone High Crosses that copy many metalwork designs. On the crosses, these intermingle with sculpture illustrating Bible

ABOVE: The Eagle evangelist symbol from the *Book of Durrow*, written around 700 and now preserved in the Library of Trinity College, Dublin.

TOP, RIGHT: A bronze crucifixion plaque from St. John's, near Athlone, dating from the 8th or 9th century that may have been venerated by the faithful on Good Friday.

BOTTOM, RIGHT: The Lismore crozier, made of bronze-wrapped wood, gold foil, and white *millefiori* glass, created for Nial Mac Meic Aeducain, bishop of Lismore, who died in 1113.

the creation of a new classically inspired style in both architecture and design. The craftsmanship that had "gone underground" for so many centuries was now reborn, and native Irish craftsmen and sculptors rose to the occasion to produce wonderful works in various media. This renaissance expressed itself first in architecture of a Palladian kind, with enchanting rococo stuccowork molded manually by both foreign and Irish stuccodores at places like Russborough, Co. Wicklow, in the 1740s. Later in the same century, a neoclassical style emerged, ornamented with garlands and other symmetrical floral motifs of Greek and Roman origin executed in the Adam style as seen, for instance, at Lucan House near Dublin. The exquisite interiors of these houses were fitted out with the best of Irish furniture, including tables bearing Irish porcelain, Waterford and Dublin glass, and silver which had an elegance that still speaks to us across two centuries. The tradition re-created by these craftspeople is continued in a different form in more recent times, when the echoes of old Irish art from the Stone to the Georgian Age are being reused and combined to enrich a lively community of craftworkers throughout modern Ireland.

stories where—unusually for Ireland—the human figures are carved naturalistically, suggesting a non-Irish source possibly as far away as Rome.

But the dawn of our own millennium saw a revival of quality in Irish metalwork, much of it in the form of shrines containing relics of Irish saints whom pilgrims would have come to venerate in the old Irish monasteries. A typical and particularly fine example is the crozier-shrine of c. 1100 discovered in the wall of Lismore Castle, Co. Waterford, in 1814; on it the animal ornament and enamel decoration of earlier centuries is revived, yet given a new contemporary twist. In the twelfth century, Irish stonemasons once more came into their own with the erection of Romanesque churches on which they carved obscure but imaginative beasts and human masks as part of round-headed doorways such as that marking the burial place of St.

Brendan the Navigator at Clonfert in Co. Galway. That doorway, of c. 1200, was the last high point but also the swan song of the art and architectural sculpture of the old Irish monasteries, for their lifeblood waned and drained with the advent of the reforming Cistercian order in the twelfth century. Their decline marked the end of that individualistic Irish art that had gone its own way for six centuries and had created a character instantly recognizable and very different from anything on the European continent. Until, and even after, the Reformation, there were a few pieces of metalwork that almost came near to the old styles and standards but, on the whole, Irish art from the thirteenth to the sixteenth century was little more than a pale reflection of the art and architecture of the Continent and that of the Norman/English conquerors of Ireland.

The seventeenth century was so riven by wars that few artistic commissions materialized, and what little there was rarely rose much above the

level of folk art, no matter how admirable that in itself may be. In the eighteenth century, however, the emergence of a new and prosperous landed gentry, largely of English origin and collectively called the Ascendancy, brought with it

I ANCIENT SITES

Only the chance discovery by the archaeologist's spade can unearth the dwelling places of Ireland's first farmers—huts mainly of wood and thatch, oppressively dark and smoky, and with not a convenience of modern-day standards in sight. In total contrast with these ephemeral and so easily destructible houses of the living are the earliest surviving houses of the dead, impressive stone piles where the bones of ancestors could find rest and be revered as the remains of pioneers who won the land they were built on, and kept it for their descendants.

These are the megalithic tombs—above-ground burial sites built of large and sometimes massive stones, which speak volumes about the ability of Stone Age man to utilize his primitive technology with the utmost skill. One can but wonder how capstones of twenty or thirty tons seem to have been maneuvered into place with such apparent ease; to stay there balancing for thousands of years with the poise and grace of a ballerina. They were erected to inspire awe in their contemporaries, and they continue to demand our admiration and respect today.

These great stone graves come in various shapes and sizes. Best known are the passage graves, so-called because a passage leads from the tomb entrance into the central burial chamber under a large, hemispherical mound, usually placed in a prominent location on the top of a hill from where it could have been seen for miles around. In principle, they share the idea of the passage and the roughly central tomb with the more famous pyramids of Egypt, each entombing a pharaoh, though differing in significant details such as the shape of the mound and the presence of multiple burials as well as date and decoration. It comes sometimes as a surprise to realize that Irish passage graves may be half a millennium or more older than the pyramids, making particular examples such as Newgrange or Knowth into some of the world's earliest architectural masterpieces. They were built by ingenious masons and craftsmen who knew how to play with stone, and how to lay out a massive mound involving hundreds of thousands of tons of material covering a carefully planned passage and tomb, and needing an army of toiling men to complete it.

Irish passage graves had no sphinx keeping watch outside, but they did have equally enigmatic ornament of rounded and angular motifs carved into the stones before they were put in place—double and triple spirals, lozenges, zigzags, usually abstract in character and copied perhaps from wood and tapestry designs that might well have decorated the houses of the living. But here they were rendered in permanent stone to make the dead feel at home for eternity. On rare occasions, the stylized form of the human face can be espied, coming to life like Don Giovanni's Commendatore, but casting a more benign and quizzical glance at us across the centuries. What would we give to get those mute and glorious characters to speak to us? Sometimes the spiral ornament is reminiscent of that in Malta and Mycenae, and one of the latter's most famous tombs, known as The Treasury of Atreus, is a perfected and meticulously chiselled version of the somewhat more raw, barbaric passage graves such as Newgrange—but built more than a thousand years later.

Rather simpler are the dolmens, monuments we can grasp at a glance, and which have an instant appeal with up to seven stones rising skywards to carry one or two capstones, an ensemble which vies for effect with the best of modern abstract sculpture. Some may have been covered by a mound of earth originally, but others were not, leaving the stones to make their stark and monumental statement on their own..

If we were faced with building a dolmen ourselves today without block-and-tackle or the help of a crane, we could very quickly form the impression that it must have been a race of giants who built these muscular monuments. Certainly they were giants in achievement—the Stone Age version of those who send rockets into space today. But, as a people, they are much more likely to have been comparatively small in stature, not nourished for growth as we are today. That sturdy folk are the basic stock of people of modern Ireland, and ongoing research in DNA may well demonstrate that theirs was the strongest contribution of all to the Irish gene pool, which was later enriched by other races. Time has told and time will tell.

What language these Stone Age inhabitants of Ireland spoke none of us will ever know. It seems unlikely that it was connected with the Gaelic branch of the Celtic language that was spoken when St. Patrick and others brought Christianity and literacy to Ireland around the fifth century of our era. But it may well have been in the Bronze Age, which followed on the Stone Age shortly before 2000 B.C., that people, speaking an ancestor of that Gaelic language still spoken in parts of Ireland today, began to come into the country, probably in comparatively small numbers. They were the people whom the Greeks called Keltoi, known to us as the Celts who were masters of half of Europe before the Romans appeared. The degree to which the sites of Ireland's Bronze Age (which lasted until around 500 B.C.) can truly be described as Celtic is a question to which there is no ready answer. Certainly, the Bronze Age people were less ostentatious in death than their Stone Age predecessors—they buried their dead underground, leaving little trace except for a low round earthen mound.

But the traces that they have left above ground include stone circles, many of which doubtless date to the Bronze Age. Sometimes found singly, though occasionally in groups (as at Beaghmore in Co. Tyrone), these circles are enigmatic. Unlike the megalithic tombs, there is little ancient folklore attached to their invention or use. Rare examples, with a single stone standing upright outside the circle, were, however, explained away in the Puritan days of the seventeenth century as a pirouette of dancers who were changed into stone along with their piper, who stood and played just outside the circle—and why? Because they had dared to dance and make merry on the Sabbath. Who knows, the circles may once have served the purpose of a meeting place for merriment, but the round shape of the circle itself could suggest that it may have played a role as a place of worship for the sun—the deity probably glorified by the passage grave builders of Newgrange and elsewhere. It has been suggested, and not without reason, that these stone circles may have functioned as primitive observatories where the movement of celestial bodies was studied. Ideas in prehistory can rarely be proved right, but it is equally difficult to demonstrate that they are wrong.

The monumental sites that greet us from the last thousand years before Christ are of a rather different kind— equally enigmatic perhaps, but also more defensive, more threatening, and suggesting the rise of a new sense of military and religious power wielding the sword to dominate the more peaceful and pastoral people living in the countryside. Symptomatic of this is the emergence of the hill-fort, a large wall adapting itself to the terrain beneath the brow of a mountain, and difficult to defend without a considerable army, though also serving perhaps as an annual tribal meeting place. But a site like Dun Aengus on the Aran Islands that keeps enemies at bay by the steep drop

in an Atlantic cliff on one side, and a series of stout walls on the other, looks altogether more defensive. Tantalizingly little is known about its history, but many other large forts of earth and stone were to become important tribal centers lasting at least down to the dawn of Irish history at the time of St. Patrick. Navan Fort at Armagh was one such place, home of the Ulaid tribe and its legendary king Conor Mac Nessa, who was protected by the youthful hero Cú Chulainn, and site of a spectacular sacrificial immolation over two thousand years ago. It was the cradle of Ulster power with a record of habitation covering seven centuries. An even more coveted prize was the Hill of Tara in Co. Meath which, even when abandoned around the sixth century A.D., played an important role as the symbolic seat of the High Kings of Ireland. One clan that claimed that title, at times at least with virtual success, were the Uí Néill, a royal family now better known as the O'Neills, whose different branches fought for domination in the northern half of Ireland for full five hundred years. One of their main northern bases—the Grianán of Aileach in Co. Donegal—provides a magnificent view over the estuaries of Foyle and Swilly.

What little we can surmise of the early history of those places would suggest that a priestly class, druids by another name, would seem to have been combining politics with religion, and probably having close ritual relationships with the powers of nature, such as water springs, later to be

Christianized as holy wells. Decorated stones may have played a role in their ritual, clearly phallic in the case of The Stone of Destiny at Tara, but it is better left to each one's imagination what the decoration on stones like that from Castlestrange were meant to symbolize.

The pagan gods, including Samuel Ferguson's "Crom crach and his sub-gods twelve," were probably fairly harmless deities more loved than feared, and that may well be why St. Patrick succeeded in replacing them so bloodlessly with his single Christian God of love and charity. He brought with him, too, the literacy of the Christian gospel. Hitherto, the only alphabet practiced in Ireland was a curious cipher called Ogham, indicating the letters by between one and five notches placed on, beside, or diagonally astride a central line, usually formed by a vertical edge on an upright stone. It was used for inscriptions commemorating individuals and their ancestors—making sure that their roots were recorded, even if we can scarcely identify now a single historically known personage among the names mentioned in the many hundreds of Ogham inscriptions that survive.

But the introduction of the Bible in written form provided an easier replacement in the shape of the Latin alphabet. This the Irish took quickly to their hearts and learned the language associated with it which, though for them a foreign tongue, gave access to a much wider international world of Latin culture denied them because Ireland had remained outside the Roman Empire. But it was from the dying embers of that self-same empire that the Irish picked up their love of Latin learning and literature, which they were later to pass back to the European continent at the court of Carolingian emperors, leading John Henry, Cardinal Newman, to coin the phrase that "Ireland was the store-house of the past and the birthplace of the future"—that future being the culture of medieval Europe, and the cradle of our modern civilization.

OPPOSITE AND RIGHT: Newgrange, overlooking the river Boyne about five miles upstream from Drogheda, has become known far beyond the bounds of Ireland since it was discovered that the rising sun shines into the darkest recesses of its passage grave on the day of the winter solstice, December 21. This happening must have been central to the design of the whole tomb-structure, as the builders created a special opening above the doorway, behind the beautifully decorated entrance stone, so as to allow the sun's rays to penetrate at a sufficiently high level along the upward-sloping passage *(left)* to illuminate the burial chamber. What a moment it must have been after the "opening ceremony" some five thousand years ago when the elite members of the community entered the burial chamber and saw how the sun's magic dispelled the darkness, its pencil-thin ray of light moving along the passage and then returning them once more to their mysterious primeval gloom when it disappeared as silently as it had come a mere seventeen minutes earlier. For the living more than the dead, the message must have meant that there was, literally in our modern parlance, light at the end of the tunnel, and that, in the same way that nature renews itself after the shortest day of the year, for mankind there is a new beginning after death—surely one of the earliest and most eloquent testimonies to a belief in the afterlife. At the inner end of that tunnel, the sun would have illumined not only the central chamber itself but also the three side-niches leading off it, one *(opposite)* with a triple-spiral (doubtless also symbol-laden) and another with a stone basin on the floor and a highly decorated roof stone.

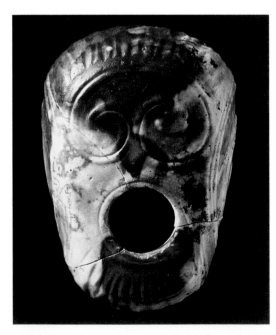

Knowth, Dowth, and Newgrange form a trio of passage graves dominating a low ridge running east-west along the northern side of the river Boyne, creating a kind of sacred landscape when they were built about three thousand years before Christ. Knowth surprised the world when, in 1967 and 1968 respectively, it was shown to have not one, but two large tombs almost back-to-back under the great mound. The kerb-stones that formed the framework of the mound are decorated with carvings that make Knowth the richest treasury of Stone Age carvings anywhere in Europe. *(Above)* One of the kerb-stones near the entrance to the eastern of the two tombs had, in addition to spiral decoration, something that looks suspiciously like a modern sundial, even down to the small hole for the gnomon. But whether or not it ever served that purpose we will never know. *(Left)* Within the eastern tomb-chamber was found one of the most astonishing manifestations of passage grave art—a superbly modeled flint mace-head, one face of which is carved in the shape of a human head, where the wide-open circular mouth would once have been occupied by a long-lost wooden handle. The particular variant of the spiral shape forming the eyes looks forward to similar designs used in Celtic art almost three thousand years later. *(Far left)* Stylization of the human face is rare but not entirely absent in passage grave art, and one other occurrence is also found at Knowth where two owl-like eyes preside over a pattern of boxed rectangles to produce a stylized smile few caricaturists could better.

OPPOSITE: The dolmen known as Poulnabrone, the hole of the sorrows, is in the midst of Ireland's lunar-like karst limestone landscape in the Burren area of north Clare. There, its stark outline has stood against the skyline since it was built sometime between 3800 and 3200 B.C., when sixteen adults and children were buried inside it.

Dolmens are among the most timeless, yet sculpturally striking, of all the Stone Age megalithic tombs of Ireland. In more senses than one, they uplift the landscape they inhabit, sometimes in a scenic location as at Gortnavern, Co. Donegal *(below)* where the dolmen stands like a faithful watchdog close to the Burnside river, looking out towards the distant Atlantic lapping the shores of Mulroy Bay. Like many another of its kind, this dolmen is dubbed Diarmaid and Gráinne's Bed in local folklore, recalling the old tale of Gráinne, who eloped with her youthful beau and had him build a new nuptial bed (the dolmen!) each night in their headlong flight from the wrath of his aging warrior-lord to whom she had been listlessly betrothed. This was none other than Fionn Mac Cumhail, a legendary hero in his earlier days, who finally caught up with Diarmaid and let him be killed by a boar on Benbulben Hill *(page 87)*. Today, that hill overlooks the grave of W. B. Yeats, who (together with George Moore) dramatized the tale for the Irish Literary Theatre (forerunner of the Abbey) in 1901. Better luck should attend you at Proleek Dolmen *(right)* in the grounds of the Ballymascanlon Hotel north of Dundalk. There, legend avers, your wish will come true if you succeed in throwing up a stone that stays on top of the dolmen.

There is a magic about the rolling well-tilled landscape of West Cork, where the stone circle at Drombeg may well have been a prehistoric center for the cult of the sun that benignly shines upon it. Excavations in the seventeen-stone circle revealed the cremated bones of a youth at its center which may date from shortly before the time of Christ, though the circle itself may be hundreds if not thousands of years older.

PAGES 26-27: Turf-cutting revealed a number of Bronze Age stone circles beneath the bog at Beaghmore, near Cookstown, in Co. Tyrone. Though not great in stature, they represent the greatest cluster of such circles known anywhere in Ireland.

LEFT: Steep sea-cliffs were a great means of defense in ancient Ireland, sparing builders the job of building walls. The greatest example is Dun Aengus on the Aran island of Inishmore in Galway Bay, where a two-hundred-foot drop to the sea protects one-half of a circle, defended by a multiple set of roughly semicircular walls. These are most likely to have been built at various times during the last millennium before Christ—the earliest occupation within the enclosure dating from around 800 B.C. Tradition says that Aengus, after whom the dún or fort is named, was a leader of the Fir Bolg tribe (probably related to the Belgae of Belgium, whom Caesar overcame), which was banished westwards from the eastern part of Ireland until it could go no farther, and entrenched itself on top of this cliff that looks out over the wide Atlantic.

OPPOSITE: Navan Fort, two miles from Armagh, was one of Ireland's most sacred sites, seat of the Red Branch Knights under the patronage of Conor Mac Nessa, king of the Ulaid tribe from which the present province of Ulster gets its name. Inhabited from around 700 B.C., it became an extraordinary cult center in 94 B.C., when a large "totem" pole was erected at the center of four ever-widening circles of further poles. All of these were later covered by stones and set alight in one gigantic ritual conflagration, and afterwards covered with an earthen mound that was excavated and then reconstituted in its present form in the 1970s. The most unexpected find was the head of a Barbary ape from Africa, which was probably brought as a diplomatic present to a king who ruled from the site sometime around the third or second century B.C.

The harp that once through Tara's halls
The soul of music shed
Now hangs as mute on Tara's walls
As if that soul were fled.
So sleeps the pride of former days
So glory's thrill is o'er
And hearts that once beat high for praise
Now feel that pulse no more.

Thomas Moore's famous verse reflects the vanished splendor of what was once the symbolic seat of the High Kings of Ireland. Already hallowed by the presence of a Stone Age passage grave, Tara became a center of power for domineering priest-kings in the centuries before the dawn of Irish history, when this panoramic hill overlooking the fruitful plains of Meath had a wall built around its fringe. This encloses a number of circular earthworks, one of which—seen here on the left—was associated by tradition with the legendary king Cormac Mac Airt. The battle of wits which St. Patrick is said to have gained over Tara's druids would have contributed to the peaceful introduction of Christianity into Ireland, and it is traditionally believed that it was the curse of another saint—Ruadhán of Lorrha—that finally led to the abandonment of the hill as a royal residence a hundred years later. But, though deserted, Tara for many centuries symbolized the High Kingship of Ireland—a consummation sought by many and gained by very few—and it kept its fabulous reputation down to the nineteenth century when Tom Moore wrote his ballad, and Daniel O'Connell used its ancient aura to gather half a million people on the hill for a nationalist rally calling for Ireland's independence.

RIGHT: The Grianán of Aileach is an imposing circular fort crowning an eight-hundred-foot-high hill overlooking the alluvial plains of Lough Swilly in Co. Donegal. Its name means the sunny place of Aileach, the name of an old kingdom comprising roughly the modern county of Donegal, and the place served as the capital of a branch of the northern Uí Néill dynasty, who ruled from here. We do not know if it was already abandoned, retaining only a symbolic significance, when it was invaded in 1101 by an O'Brien king of Munster who, according to tradition, ordered each of his soldiers to take away a stone from the fort with them. His army cannot have been too large, for they left enough stones there for Bishop Barnard of Derry to restore it to its present appearance in the nineteenth century.

RIGHT: The stone at Castlestrange in Co. Roscommon is no petrified dodo's egg, but one of only five examples in Ireland of domed boulders intricately decorated with designs in the La Tène style of the Celts, and dating from the last few centuries before Christ. Its precise significance has long been lost, and all we can do now is to presume that it was once a prominent symbol in the religious ritual of pagan Ireland.

BELOW: The Ogham stone at Dunmore Head near the end of the Dingle Peninsula, not far from Dunquin, for Irishmen "the next parish to America," is located in an area where the everyday language of the people is some of the most beautiful Gaelic spoken today. Just offshore are the Blasket Islands, where there was a tremendous Gaelic literary flowering during the first half of this century. The Ogham stones are appropriately the earliest surviving specimens of that same language, widely used from the fourth to the eighth centuries. Their inscriptions, formed by letters made of notches on the edges of upright stones, commemorate individuals and their ancestors. This one (with notches visible near the stone's top left) recalls a man named Erc who, sadly, cannot be historically identified, though he may well have been the owner of the fortified promontory on which the stone stands.

OPPOSITE: Similar in style to the Grianán of Aileach, though never even mentioned in historical sources, is Staigue Fort, situated in a hauntingly beautiful valley on the Iveragh peninsula (better known as The Ring of Kerry), where it looks down towards an inlet of the Atlantic Ocean.

OPPOSITE: The ancient Irish used promontories by the sea to fortify themselves, the steep cliff-faces on three sides making it necessary to defend only the landward end. On the promontory at Dunbeg on the Dingle Peninsula, one stone wall and three earthen banks protect a single stone house inside. The walls and banks may date to prehistoric times, but the house may be no earlier than the tenth century A.D. Sadly, as is so often the case with Ireland's ancient monuments, history is silent about its builders.

ABOVE, LEFT AND RIGHT: One of the great advantages of the rocky countryside of the West of Ireland is that it encouraged so much building in stone, thus helping monuments to survive that would have long since disintegrated had they been built in wood. To describe as a fort a stone structure such as Leacanabuaile on The Ring of Kerry is perhaps a misnomer, for such a place could scarcely keep an army at bay for more than a few minutes, and it is more likely to have been a family farm, or even a haven for pilgrims. The oldest building at Leacanabuaile is the round house close to the back wall opposite the entrance, and the square house in the center was added somewhat later, probably sometime during the sixth to the eighth centuries A.D.

II STONE MONASTERIES AND ABBEYS

Early medieval Ireland differed much from the rest of Europe in that its main ecclesiastical centers were not bishoprics but monasteries. St. Patrick's church was probably diocesan in character but it was in the sixth century, less than a hundred years after his day, that the monasteries began to flourish, and quickly spread over the country like a field of daisies. Founded by saints on land usually donated by a local king or potentate—whose descendants frequently claimed the abbacy—the monasteries became, in time, the fosterers of culture, history, and art and remained so for another six hundred years. It is they that we have to thank for the milieu that produced the *Books of Durrow* and *Kells,* the chalices of Ardagh and Derrynaflan, and important compilations such as the twelfth-century *Lebor na hUidre* (or *Book of the Dun Cow*) and the *Book of Leinster*, which preserve for us so much of ancient Irish lore and law.

One of the earliest of the great abbots was Finnian of Clonard in Co. Meath; his monastery became a "nursery of saints" who went out themselves and made new foundations of their own, men like Ciarán of Clonmacnoise, Columba of Iona, Brendan of Clonfert (the great navigator), and Ruadhán of Lorrha, who cursed Tara.

Probably the greatest of them was St. Columba (521–597), called Colm Cille in Irish, who was the first of the Irish monks to leave his country on voluntary pilgrimage to spread the word of the Lord and to found monasteries like that on the island of Iona in the inner Hebrides. From there, his monks went on to bring Christianity to certain parts of northern Britain, while the European continent beckoned to others like St. Columbanus who contributed greatly to the spread of the monastic spirit through foundations such as Luxeuil in France and Bobbio in northern Italy. His was one of a number of monastic rules which laid down guidelines for the monastic life, which was very harsh, with even the smallest of peccadillos severely punished. Some took it upon themselves to be even more extreme in becoming hermits, often on lake or sea-girth islands, where they could pray in greater peace and quiet. Such was the spirituality of those men—and presumably women, though we hear all too little of them— that they communicated with their Maker through an appreciation of the natural world around them which He had created. They were among the first to write a vernacular (that is, non-Latin) poetry anywhere in Europe. Preserved for us in the form of inspired verse often written on the margins of their manuscripts, these poems were beautiful invocations of the world of the birds and the bees, like the following brief verses translated by the late Máire Mac Neill:

Over me green branches hang
A blackbird leads the loud song;
Above my pen-lined booklet
I hear a fluting bird-throng.

The cuckoo pipes a clear call
Its dun cloak hid in deep dell;
Praise to God for this goodness
That in woodland I write well.

In time, certain monasteries became preeminent: Armagh (which started its life as a bishopric), Kildare (site of St. Brigid's double monastery for monks and nuns), and Clonmacnoise, which owed its importance to being at the crossroads of Ireland and to getting patronage from kings of the western province of Connacht who were buried there. But fame and riches took their toll on the religious spirit of these monasteries—some went to war with others, leaving many dead upon the field of battle, and moral laxity became the norm. Efforts towards reform came in the late eighth century, but only with limited success, and though they survived the monk-bashing raids of the Viking Norse in the following hundred years, it was, paradoxically, the reform movement of the twelfth century, spearheaded in Ireland by Malachy the saintly bishop of Armagh, which finally brought about their decline, replacing them with new monasteries with stricter ideals founded by Cistercians and Augustinians.

When we visit their sites today, it is difficult to conceive what these monasteries originally looked like. The clutter of modern tombstones replaces the small wooden cells of the monks, and the focal point would have been a wooden church, usually surrounded by an earthen bank within which both innocent and guilty could claim the right of sanctuary. The monastery at Nendrum, Co. Down, shows two other walls outside the central one, suggesting that monasteries would have had concentric enclosures—an innermost sanctuary for church and monks, a second for craftspeople who were not monks, and a third perhaps for enclosing vegetable gardens and tilled fields. The monasteries became, in effect, small towns with populations, both lay and secular,

who were involved in craftwork and agriculture as well as in the teaching of religion. Books were copied in scriptoria, the Bible was read and commented upon, the Psalms were sung daily, and the learning these monasteries possessed they shared with others both at home and abroad. Hordes flocked from England and France to benefit from the freely given education, and Irish monks went to the European continent where they were much in demand as teachers and exegetes, like the great neo-Platonist philosopher Johannes Scottus Eriugena ("Irish born"), who astounded the Carolingian court with his knowledge of Greek.

There is little or nothing on the old monastic sites today which will bring us back visually or in spirit to the days of the founding fathers in the sixth century, for what we now find there in the way of ancient monuments—churches, Round Towers, High Crosses, or cross-decorated memorial slabs—are scarcely any earlier than the ninth century. But they are, each in their own way, remarkable contributions to the art and architecture of early medieval Europe and, though towers and crosses may not be exclusive to Ireland, the country undoubtedly preserves the best examples.

OPPOSITE, TOP AND BOTTOM: Few places evoke the hard and ascetic nature of early Irish monasticism better than Skellig Michael, an island eight miles off the southwest coast of Kerry. There are two Skellig islands, the lesser of the two—a gannet colony—being visible in all the pictures here. On the greater Skellig island, what are normally taken to be the remains of an ancient monastery perch on a ledge some 560 feet above sea level and are dedicated, not surprisingly, to St. Michael the archangel, patron saint of high places. A steep stairs *(opposite, bottom)* leads up to the terraced monastic enclosure where a pillar carved with a cross on one face *(opposite, top)* bears an uncanny resemblance to a cowled monk viewed from behind. Skellig Michael was where Sir Kenneth Clark, the historian of civilization, envisioned Christianity clinging for survival on the western periphery of Europe while the rest of the continent was overrun by barbarian invasions in the fifth and sixth centuries. However, in due time Skellig Michael itself was invaded by barbarians in the shape of the Vikings, who caused the death of a Skellig monk, though one of them—a king of Norway no less—later had himself baptized by a hermit of the island.

BELOW: On the perilous slopes of Skellig Michael, and up the steep flight of steps from the sea, monks toiled to create a series of terraces on which there were at least seven beehive huts of stone *(below)* and two further small oratories, all built without the use of mortar. Because an abbot of Skellig is mentioned in the old Irish annals, we must presume that there was a monastery on the island, but the question may well be posed if a community could survive a whole winter in isolation on this bleak spot with little more to eat than the flesh and eggs of gannets who breed on the inhospitable neighboring island of Little Skellig. Four raids by Vikings between 812 and 839 would indicate that there must have been valuables worth looting on the island, suggesting that any monastic settlement there might have preserved some precious reliquaries. But consider an alternative suggestion for the use of the beehive huts, namely as hostels for pilgrims who came to say their prayers and venerate the relics but who may have had to stay on the island longer than expected to wait for a favorable wind to waft them back to the mainland. Evidence attests that Skellig Michael was a much-famed place of pilgrimage at least as late as the seventeenth century.

ABOVE: Gallarus Oratory, near the end of the Dingle Peninsula in Co. Kerry, is the most perfect of a group of twenty or so of its kind built along the west coast of Ireland sometime between 700 and 1200 A.D. Its corbel method of construction is adapted from that of the round beehive huts, and the superb mortarless masonry of Gallarus has ensured that its long walls have not fallen in, as is the case with so many others. Its shape has been compared to an upturned boat or a turf-stack, and light only gets in through the sloping-sided door and a small round-headed window. For Seamus Heaney, Ireland's most recent Nobel Prize–winning poet, it is like "a core of old dark walled up with stone a yard thick."

RIGHT: The small island of Saint MacDara off the coast of Connemara in Co. Galway is the venue for a local festival on July 16th each year when boatloads sail out to the island to celebrate the saint's feast day. Their focus is a beautiful oratory with very large stones for such a small building, and whose stone roof and projecting gables, together with its finials (modern replacements), betray an imitation of a wooden church. The great twelfth-century French Cistercian Bernard of Clairvaux remarked that the Irish were building wooden churches in his day, three hundred years after stone churches had begun to become common in Ireland, and he was probably right in attributing this custom to the innately conservative nature of the Irish building tradition. Certainly, Saint MacDara's church could be regarded as somewhat old-fashioned for a building that is roughly contemporary with St. Bernard, and very much smaller than those to which he was accustomed, but its masonry and simple, lintelled doorway make it into a timeless creation that Paul Caponigro, the great American photographer, described as an "exquisitely proportioned building" and an "archetype in stone."

OPPOSITE: The long, low island of Inishmurray off the Sligo coast preserves a remarkable number of traces of early Christian faith in Ireland—churches, cross-decorated slabs on isolated piles of stone, and, most striking of all, an oval enclosure surrounded by a high stone wall or *caiseal*. Inside it, the area is divided up into separate sections by low cross-walls. In one is a small stone-roofed oratory called after the monastic founder, Molaisse, whose thirteenth-century wooden statue was preserved within before being removed for safety to the National Museum of Ireland some fifty years ago. The richness of the decorated stonework on the island is best explained by what we may presume to have been its former importance as a place of pilgrimage, which it retained until the last inhabitants left the island in 1948. Interestingly, one of the buildings within the enclosure is a beehive hut, like those of Skellig Michael, and it may have been dedicated to St. Brendan, the navigator who may have reached America centuries before Leif Ericsson, and who was probably the patron of maritime pilgrimage up and down the west coast of Ireland in the early medieval period. The enclosure probably contained buildings of wood in earlier times which have long since disintegrated.

No self-respecting Irish monastery was without its Round Tower as a kind of status symbol, and it served as such in the last century when Irish nationalists associated Round Towers with the Golden Age of monastic Ireland. Built between 950 and 1200, these tapering towers with their conical tops are best likened to a pared pencil standing on its flattened end. With only two exceptions out of about sixty-five known examples, the doorways, like that at Glendalough (*left*), are usually about ten feet above the ground—to make access difficult in times of danger, it was thought. But such towers would have been ill-suited for defense, as an internal fire caused by a blazing arrow would have created an inferno out of the wooden stairs leading to the top—and anyone or thing inside. The old Irish word for these towers was *cloigthech,* or bell-house, linking them in style with the campanile of Italy and the minaret of the Muslim world. But, as a bell was an item apparently borne by Irish pilgrims, the towers may have facilitated them in some way. The upper part of the tower is the first the modern traveler sees of Glendalough, and, in ages past, it may have encouraged them to step with renewed vigor towards their goal.

ABOVE: The ancient monastery of Ardmore ("the great height") stands like a watchdog above the Celtic sea on the southern coast of Co. Waterford, and a slender Round Tower is its beacon. The site must be one of the oldest Christian foundations in the country, as its patron saint is Declan, reputed to have been one of the four saints in Ireland before Patrick. Its cathedral, from *c.* 1200, is dominated by the graceful twelfth-century tower that rises to a height of ninety feet, its rocket-like aspirations toward heaven brought somewhat down to earth, as it

were, by the horizontal string courses creating three unequal stages in the body of the tower.

OPPOSITE: Tucked away in the Wicklow mountains is the Valley of the Two Lakes, better known as Glendalough, an early Irish monastery founded by St. Kevin, who died in 618, of whom the poet Samuel Lover (1797–1868) wrote:

At Glendalough lived a young saint,
In odour of sanctity dwelling,
An old-fashioned odour, which now
We seldom or never are smelling.

Each of the two lakes is the focus of churches associated with the monastery, but the center was below the lower lake where St. Kevin probably lies buried. Close to the Round Tower on the right is the now-ruined cathedral, Ireland's second largest building to survive from before the twelfth century. Few, if any, of the other smaller churches are likely to predate 1000, and some are probably the result of the building activity of Glendalough's second—and Ireland's first formally canonized— saint, Laurance O'Toole, who was abbot here before becoming archbishop of Dublin in 1163.

Glendalough has the soubriquet "of the seven churches"—and one of these, St. Kevin's (on the left), is unique because a small Round Tower projects above the western end of its stone roof. Where the ground is now covered in tombstones, originally there would have been wooden huts for the monks, which must have been quite numerous, to judge by a report of 1177 that tells of a flash flood that left fish strewn around the streets, indicating a settlement of considerable size.

OPPOSITE: The Rock of Cashel is the most stunning cluster of ancient monuments to survive from medieval Ireland. Rising dramatically out of the Golden Vale in Co. Tipperary, it is reputedly the site where St. Patrick baptized an early king of Munster and, by mistake, put his crozier butt through the foot of the king who bore the pain without flinching because he thought it was part of the baptismal ceremony!

The Rock was, indeed, the seat of the MacCarthy kings of Munster until 1101, when it was handed over to the Church which shortly afterwards started to build on it. In addition to the well-preserved Round Tower, the earliest structure on the Rock is Cormac's Chapel, consecrated with great pomp and circumstance in 1134. It is Ireland's first and only real piece of Romanesque architecture, with its unusual twin square towers in place of transepts, and stone roof rising up above the blind-arcaded walls, all fashioned in warmly glowing sandstone. Almost cradling but also dwarfing it is the thirteenth-century Gothic cathedral, looking more severe with contrasting limestone walls of colder grey, and with its nave truncated before completion to form a fortified archbishop's residence. A twelfth-century cross, thought to feature a figure of St. Patrick on one face, is now preserved in the recently restored Hall of the Vicars' Choral (low on the left), a two-story building which now serves as a museum close to the entrance.

ABOVE AND RIGHT: Though now standing alone in the midst of the Irish countryside, Clonmacnoise was once a bustling monastic town at the very center of Ireland, situated at a crossroads where the north-south-flowing Shannon was an important traffic artery crossed by a bridge carrying the country's main east-west roadway. Apart from its advantageous location, its fame rested on the sanctity of its founder, St. Ciarán (512–545), who may have spent only the last year of his short life here, but whose charisma still encourages people to come to this magnetic site down to our own day. The oldest-known site of Christian pilgrimage in Ireland, its most famous pilgrim was Pope John Paul II, who chose Clonmacnoise as the only old Irish monastery to visit during his brief stay in Ireland in 1979. Its cathedral was the largest church edifice built in Ireland before 1100, and through its later Gothic window one can catch a glimpse of one of the site's Round Towers, built into the Romanesque church of St. Finghin. Clonmacnoise also has another Round Tower, built only a few decades earlier in the 1120s. In addition to the cathedral and St. Finghin's, the monastery had other churches, including Temple Dowling *(above, in the background)*, which gets its name from Edward Dowling who extended the church in 1689 and inserted a plaque over the doorway to record his activity.

Royal patronage encouraged Clonmacnoise to develop into one of Ireland's richest monasteries. Its wealth is intimated in the list of items detailed in The Annals of Clonmacnoise as having been stolen in 1125, including a model of the Temple of Solomon, a silver cup, a gilt cross, a silver chalice, and various jewels, which had been bestowed upon the church by kings from Meath and Connacht, as well as by the archbishop of Armagh. But such gifts and wealth allowed Clonmacnoise to become also one of Ireland's great artistic centers, though none of its metalwork or manuscripts are still preserved in situ. What do remain, however, as testimonies of its artistic capabilities, are a number of High Crosses of stone, including the ninth-century South Cross *(see above)*, now in the on-site Interpretative Center.

The High Cross can be regarded as the embodiment of the spirit of early Celtic monasticism in Ireland. These tall stone crosses, with the ring embracing and holding the arms in place and acting as a cosmic symbol around the representation of the crucified Christ, have their surfaces covered in carving illustrating Bible stories and enlivened by additional abstract geometrical designs.

Of the hundreds of stone crosses surviving in Ireland from the ninth and tenth centuries, some eighty-five or so bear figure sculpture—and the best are preserved on old monastic sites in the midlands and east of the country. One of those with a goodly collection of crosses is Clonmacnoise, where, in addition to the South Cross (*page 43*), there is the even more attractive Cross of the Scriptures (*left*), probably identical with one mentioned in historical sources in the year 1060. Its ring, unusually, stands out in relief from the cross itself with its uptilting arms, and its numerous panels carved with figures tell the story of Christ's passion, death, and resurrection and, on the side shown here, his role as Judge on the Last Day.

At the North Cross at Ahenny, Co. Tipperary (*opposite*), the figures are confined to the base, while the shaft shines forth with a delicate gossamer of geometrical ornament copying metalwork and probably assignable to the ninth century.

ABOVE: Built into a wall of the ruined church on White Island in Lower Lough Erne, Co. Fermanagh, are a number of curious figures which have excited inquisitiveness and imagination for generations. We know that they belong to the Christian era because one of them, armed with sword and shield, carries on his shoulder a brooch of "Tara" type, which can be no earlier than the eighth century A.D. Of equal size is its neighbor holding in each hand a duck-headed quadruped. Rather larger in scale is a female carrying a staff and bell (abbess or pilgrim?), and another figure (male or female?) putting one hand to the mouth (a gesture of silence?). The attributes and differing sizes of the figures pose problems of interpretation: what are they doing, why the differing grimaces, who are they and what do they represent? Were they part of church furniture, supporting the rising steps for a pulpit for instance, or supports for the reliquary-shrine of some long-forgotten saint? They challenge our historical imagination as they keep their secret still.

RIGHT: Lower Lough Erne in Co. Fermanagh has another intriguing sculpture mystery, where we cannot even be sure whether it is pagan or Christian—the two-headed figure on Boa Island, Seamus Heaney's "god-eyed sex-mouthed stone." That inscrutable look, the bearded face, the folded arms across the breast, a belted garment, and hair on the sides intertwined with that of another head back-to-back. What does it all mean? Is this a pagan god, with only one face less than a three-headed stone from Corleck, Co. Cavan, taken to be a Celtic god? Or an Irish version of the twin-headed Janus figures of ancient Rome? Who will ever know what the carver of this modeled block had in mind when he chiselled out that somewhat threatening mask—it was surely more than something just to keep us guessing!

PAGE 47: Built into the western gable of the twelfth- or thirteenth-century Cathedral of St. Declan at Ardmore are sculptures which, though enigmatic in parts, have other sections that help to determine what they were. In a sequence that is not original, and spread over two arches below and an arcade of niches above, the carvings include the Bible's earliest story in the form of Adam and Eve in the center of the lower left arch. At the top of its sibling on the right as we look at it is another Old Testament scene. This shows King Solomon on the left raising his sword, about to give his famous judgment as to which of the two ladies approaching him is the real mother of the child held out towards him by one of them, as a harper (David?) plays in the background. Efforts to decipher the subject matter of the other carvings have not met with universal accord, nor is it known whether they were formerly located elsewhere in the cathedral, or in another building long vanished, though they are quite likely to belong to the period of the cathedral that was built when Ardmore was seat of a diocese between 1170 and 1210.

OPPOSITE: The doorway of the Augustinian cloister at Cong in Co. Mayo (where Rory O'Connor, the last High King of Ireland, died in 1198) was carved in the 1220s by masons who adopted the latest Gothic style of pointed arch, but applied to it their more old-fashioned zig-zag ornament going back to the previous century. This is one of the last great works of what Leask called "the School of the West"—a group or workshop of superior craftsmen who produced beautifully finished masonry in a late Romanesque style after it had gone out of fashion in all but the more peripheral areas of Europe. The cloister arcade is an 1860s recreation by a talented local mason, Peter Foy, who worked for Sir Benjamin Lee Guinness, the then owner of Ashford Castle in whose grounds the abbey lies.

RIGHT: The famed Cistercian abbey of Jerpoint in Co. Kilkenny had Romanesque beginnings too in the later twelfth century, and it is to this period that much of the present church belongs, though developing more and more Gothic overtones. The large square tower—the tallest ever built by the Irish Cistercians—was an addition of the fifteenth century, as is the cloister arcade built with financial aid from the Butler Earls of Ormonde.

BELOW: The first Cistercian House to herald the reform intended to bring the lax old Irish monasteries back to the stricter ways of religious life was Mellifont in Co. Louth, founded with the assistance of St. Malachy of Armagh in 1142. In contrast to the seemingly haphazard layout of some of Ireland's earlier monasteries, the Cistercians brought with them an ordered ground-plan of a square or rectangular grassed cloister garth surrounded by an arcade and located next to a much more expansive church with large transepts. Around 1200, the monks of Mellifont built at one end of the cloister garth a beautiful two-story lavabo, once bubbling with stream-water for them to wash their hands before and after meals, and enclosed by an octagon of rounded arches delicately carved. Excavation in the 1950s unearthed enough of the roughly contemporary cloister arcade for it to be partially reconstructed nearby.

LEFT: The Black Death, or bubonic plague, of 1347–1350 took a heavy toll in the Norman towns, but also probably among the Cistercians, and by the time the Gaelic resurgence began in earnest in the early fifteenth century, their role as prime monastic builders was taken over by other orders, particularly the Franciscans, whose late medieval Gothic friaries are a particularly attractive Irish contribution to the ecclesiastical architecture of Europe. But the Augustinians too joined the new building craze and at Adare they, like the Franciscans, replaced the airy lean-to arcade of the Cistercians with a more solid structure which had another floor added above it, giving the friars' walk inside a more somber aspect.

OPPOSITE: After a lapse of hundreds of years, the Gothic style was revived in baronial mansions like that built at Kylemore by the wealthy Liverpool merchant, Mitchell Henry, M.P. (1826–1910), in the second half of the last century at an idyllic lakeside location in Connemara. Appropriately, it, too, was to become an abbey after the First World War when the Irish Dames of Ypres made it into Ireland's only Benedictine convent.

III Fortresses and Castles

It was the Irish themselves who built the first castles in the country, particularly the O'Connor kings of Connacht who wanted to boost their power and protect themselves against their fellow Irishmen in the first half of the twelfth century—though not a trace of their work survives. But the tables were soon turned when the Normans arrived in 1169/70, and within two-thirds of a century they had conquered two-thirds of the country—including the western province of Connacht—by means of superior tactics and armory, but also by building castles that would last. Their first bridgeheads were created hastily by throwing up rounded flat-topped mounds known as mottes, or square earthworks with ditch and bank, both defended by a wooden tower. Guerrilla warfare, however, soon turned their minds towards stone fortifications and, within five years, the Norman barons began to build stout towers of stone to stake their claim to the land they had recently conquered by the sword.

There is no better demonstration of Norman construction than Trim Castle *(opposite)* in Co. Meath. An initial defense of earth and wood erected in 1172 by Hugh Tyrell on behalf of his Norman overlord, Hugh de Lacy, was soon attacked and set on fire by Rory O'Connor, the king of Connacht. De Lacy retaliated speedily by erecting what is now the central donjon or tower of stone in 1174/75, a fact that has only emerged very recently from tree-ring dates provided by the wooden scaffolding used in the construction, and surviving in holes in the exterior walls. In plan, this tower is like an equal-armed Greek cross, formed of a square center with smaller towers added to each side, but providing so many outside angles too easy to undermine that the castle may have been more of a status symbol than a formidable defense. However, like Rome, the castle was not built in a day, and other pieces of wood indicate that the tower did not reach its full height until about thirty years later. Experience makes better castle builders of us all (in sand or stone!), and it was obviously found necessary to defend the castle further. Its location was made into a D-shaped island by diverting the river Boyne to create a water-filled moat around it, and its edges were protected by a long curtain wall interspersed by towers on either side.

Although the most extensive, Trim is nevertheless only one of the many castles the Normans built in the four provinces of Ireland as they tightened their grip all over the country—except in the northwest, where the Irish held out proudly against the invader until early in the seventeenth century. Before the Normans arrived, fights among the Irish were usually more skirmishes than battles, and the victor was more likely to retreat back home, satisfied at having ousted an enemy, rather than staying to occupy the loser's land permanently. But that was precisely what the Normans did when they arrived, taking possession of the land they had so recently won by the sword. The Irish were outraged by such conduct—it was not sticking to the rules of the game— but they were powerless to prevent it in the face of greater odds. It was many decades before they got their act together and fought back successfully, starting with the Battle of Calann near Kenmare in 1261. The Irish were later to be aided by the bubonic plague known as the Black Death in 1347, which devastated the urban centers of Norman power while leaving the rural Irish population comparatively unscathed.

Symptomatic of what happened next is the story of Quin Abbey in Co. Clare, where a Franciscan friary was erected in 1433 on the foundations of an old Norman castle burned to the ground by the native Irish. The fifteenth century thus saw Gaelic Ireland rising from the ashes like a phoenix, but not only

in the form of religious architecture. It was at this period, starting tentatively already in the fourteenth century, that the Irish began building new castles for themselves, creating their own status symbols to impress their friends and thumb their noses at their enemies. But these castles were different from their Norman forerunners. Trim Castle and its like had been built to house and be defended by a whole army of soldiers; in a word, a castle and barracks all in one. These new Irish castles were, as their more correct title "tower house" implies, built more for family use, and were probably defended by no more than a handful of faithful "kerne," as the Irish soldiers were called. The size and stature of these towers varied, depending on how many workmen the local landlords could press-gang into building them. But some were certainly very sizable and impressive, none more so than Blarney Castle, built allegedly by Cormac Láidir ("the strong") MacCarthy in 1446. Another equally imposing pile started shortly afterwards is Bunratty in Co. Clare, where today medieval banquets are enacted every evening, presided over by an "Earl of Thomond" for the night, in opulent surroundings with furniture, tapestries, and paintings an Irish overlord might have had in the sixteenth century.

Things were much simpler farther down the castle-builders' social scale. In the seventeenth century, a French traveler, Monsieur de la Boullaye le Gouz, described such towers as having a thatched roof, little furniture, and floors with a deep covering of rushes "with which the Irish also made their beds in summer." But if the furniture was little more than a table in the uppermost room, it was heavily laden with food and drink to provide the visitor with a hearty welcome. An Englishman, Luke Gernon, described his reception in 1620 and spoke of beer, whiskey, wine, and ale presented to him by the lady of the house who tasted them first herself before handing them to him—an offer which, he says, he daren't refuse. "'Meates" he ate ("but ill cooked without sauce"), as the harper joined the feast before the guest finally retired to his bed, which he might have shared "if the company be great!" Tower houses such as these continued to be built into the early seventeenth century, and a number of them, particularly in the West of Ireland, have been restored in recent decades *(p. 16)* to fulfill once more their original function as family homes.

Although the Irish were able to continue building the occasional castle after the collapse of Gaelic Ulster—and indeed much of Gaelic culture as well—in the first decade of the seventeenth century, the next castles to be erected were put up by new arrivals. These were people who came to plant the land taken from the defeated Irish in various parts of the country, but whose families have long since integrated themselves into Irish society and, at times, even opened up parts of their property to the public. One such instance is Birr Castle in Co. Offaly *(right)*, which was built by the Parsons family in the 1620s in the precincts of an older O'Carroll castle that had been granted to them. It was subsequently more extensively fortified by outworks in the form of pointed bastions, of a kind more easily visible from the air, and seen to best advantage in their finest display at Charles Fort near Kinsale in Co. Cork. But, a decade later, what seemed like an impregnable fortress, that bristled with cannon pointing out to sea, was conquered from the landward side by the forces of King William of Orange, whose victory over the Stuart king James II ushered in a century of grandiose country house building. It was not until the nineteenth century that castle building really came back into its own again—but this time not as fortification, but as a display of wealth and pomp, which must have stood out in strong contrast to the much more humble abodes of the majority of the Irish population.

ABOVE: Birr Castle, Co. Offaly.

OPPOSITE: Trim Castle, Co. Meath.

LEFT: As in earlier times, water was often used to strengthen defense in the medieval period by building castles on islands or headlands. Kenbane Castle on the coast of Co. Antrim is dramatically sited on an offshore islet of chalk, surrounded by shore boulders on which no ship could beach, and is reachable from the land only by a tortuous path. Walls fortify about a third of the headland, and are dominated by a small tower, probably built by the powerful MacDonald clan in the first half of the sixteenth century—its present ruined state being apparently the result of the tower having been "defaced" by Sir James Croft in 1551.

RIGHT: Ross Castle in Co. Kerry used inland waters—in this instance, the beautiful Lakes of Killarney—as part of its defenses. The castle was probably built in the early fifteenth century by the O'Donoghue Ross chieftains of the area but, after a rebellion in the 1580s, it came into the hands, first of Donal MacCarthy Mór and, later, of the Browne family. The side surrounding the lake was well fortified by an outer bawn-wall with towers, probably because, according to legend, the castle could only be taken from the water. But when the Cromwellian commander Ludlow hit upon the idea of bringing boats overland to refloat them in the Lakes of Killarney in 1652, the garrison panicked at the prospect of the old prophecy being fulfilled, and surrendered the castle, making it the last stronghold in Ireland to submit to Cromwellian forces. The castle came under threat again in the Williamite wars around 1690 and, early in the following century, a barracks was attached to it, but its roof—and the whole garrison with it—were finally removed in 1825. It is now owned by the State, which has done a magnificent service in restoring and presenting it to the public.

RIGHT AND OPPOSITE: The castles shown here are markedly different products of two of the major families in the southern province of Munster during the medieval period. The smaller one, O'Brien's Castle *(right),* on the Aran Islands in Co. Galway, now part of the province of Connacht, was in Munster territory when it was built. The islands were owned at the time by the O'Briens, descendants of the legendary king of North Munster, Brian Boru, who lost his life at the Battle of Clontarf in 1014. Around 1500, they erected this neat little tower in the stony terrain of Inisheer, the island nearest their own territorial base in Co. Clare, in the hope of controlling trade in wine in and out of the port of Galway, but it was the O'Flaherties of Galway who finally wrested the islands from the O'Briens and claimed them for Co. Galway.

On a different scale altogether is the magnificent tower at Blarney in Co. Cork *(opposite),* built by the MacCarthys—kings of South Munster—around 1446. Rising up behind the ruined turrets of an early eighteenth-century house, the tower has five stories and reaches a height of eighty-five feet. A stone beneath its parapet, when kissed on its under-surface as you lie on your back, is said to give the gift of eloquence. The origin of the custom is unknown—and the Irish may not need to practice it since they talk enough (some would even say too much) already—but since the word *blarney,* or cajoling talk, has now been a part of the English language for centuries, it has given the castle and its stone a worldwide reputation.

RIGHT: The perilous northern sea coast provides the backdrop for two of the most romantically sited castles of medieval Ireland. Doe Castle nestles near the head of Sheephaven in Co. Donegal. The MacSweeney family, masters of the territory known as Doe from which the castle gets its name, were probably its original builders around 1500, though they were later to lose it, and regain it again, a number of times. Its place in Irish history is assured because of its surprising links with Spain. Doe Castle harbored Owen Roe O'Neill, who landed there with one hundred veterans from Spain before setting off to take command of the Irish army in the bloody wars of the 1640s, and, earlier, in 1588, its welcome was extended to survivors of the Spanish Armada.

OPPOSITE: While the Spanish were recovering from their ordeal in Co. Donegal, a galleass of the Armada, the *Girona,* was shipwrecked at Lacada Point, close to Dunluce Castle on the Antrim coast, and its rescued treasures—the finest to be recovered from the disastrous maritime expedition—are now among the highlights at the Ulster Museum in Belfast. The castle itself is dramatically sited on a spit jutting out into the sea. Its earliest portions are the two rounded bastions built by the MacQuillan family, probably some time before 1400. The Macdonnells, who later gained possession, were responsible for building the rest of the castle, but it was probably abandoned for the greater safety of the adjoining solid land after the seaward end of the castle fell into the sea in 1639, taking many of the domestic staff with it to a watery grave below.

ABOVE AND RIGHT: Bunratty Castle, standing close enough to Shannon Airport so that people stopping over can visit it, is the third or fourth defense structure on the site, this present one erected by the Macnamara family around 1450. During the following century, it passed into the hands of the O'Briens, earls of Thomond, and it is the castle as it might have been in their heyday in the later sixteenth century that is splendidly presented today, serving as a backdrop to the medieval banquets that take place every evening. In 1646, the gardens and deerpark surrounding the castle were highly praised by the Papal Nuncio, Cardinal Rinuccini, who said that he had never seen a more beautiful spot. The idyll was, however, shattered later in the same year when Cromwellian forces took the castle from its defender, Admiral Penn, an event experienced perhaps by his infant son, William, who was later to become the founder of Pennsylvania.

OPPOSITE: On abandoning Bunratty, Admiral Penn headed with his family for Kinsale in Co. Cork, where, some forty years later, the most impressive fortification ever built in Ireland was nearing completion. This was Charles Fort, named after the Stuart monarch Charles II. It is a star-shaped fort with its multiple-layered fortifications modeled on the latest French ideas developed by Louis XIV's great military architect, Vauban. On paper it looked impregnable from the sea, but the decision to locate it on the shoreline proved fatal, for it had to surrender when Williamite forces attacked it with cannon from the hill behind in 1690. The barrack buildings were added to the interior in the eighteenth and nineteenth centuries, and finally abandoned in 1921.

PAGE 62: Clifden Castle, Co. Galway, is now abandoned but still retains its beautiful view down towards the sea, across the former front lawn which had been reclaimed from bog by its builder John D'Arcy, who settled here in 1815. He was the second largest landowner in Connemara in his day, and was responsible for developing its capital, the attractive town of Clifden, which also gives its name to this castle, described by the Victorian novelist W. M. Thackeray as a "fine chateau."

PAGE 63: A close invocation of the battlemented towers of the medieval period, as dreamed up by Romantic Victorians (shades of Tennyson's "the splendor falls on castle walls"), is Lismore Castle *(top)*. Its foundations go back to the early Norman period (a medieval crozier shrine of c. 1100 and the later "Book of Lismore" were found walled up in a tower there in 1814), but the impressive facade towering above the river Blackwater was the brainchild of Joseph Paxton, better known as the creator of the Crystal Palace in London. The castle is owned by the Duke of Devonshire, one of whose family married Adele Astaire, the dancer and actress, who has been a frequent visitor to the castle.

The later eighteenth century and the whole of the nineteenth saw the rejuvenation of castle building, but this time for wealthy families and no longer for defense. Slane Castle *(bottom)*, for hundreds of years the home of the Conyngham family, was rebuilt in 1785 in a classical style, from designs by the noted architect James Wyatt.

IV NATURE AND LANDSCAPE

In shape, Ireland looks something like a cuddly furry pet sitting comfortably on its hind quarters, turning its back on the engulfing ambitions of its larger sister-island to the east, and looking for attention from its other neighbor far across the ocean to the west. In fact, that continent to the west, namely North America, is on a tectonic plate that converged with Europe (in the southern hemisphere!) a mere 450 million years ago, the seam crossing what is now Ireland from the Shannon to Dundalk Bay—with American fossils to the northwest of that line, and European to the southeast. Nature let the Atlantic intervene to send them on their separate ways, leaving Ireland over aeons to become the lovable little island it is today.

In elevation, Ireland bears some comparison to a saucer, flat in the middle and higher around the edges—with mountains and hills—though with occasional breaks, for instance, north of Dublin on the east coast. These hills, reaching a maximum height of 3414 feet on the summit of Carrantuohil in the MacGillycuddy Reeks in Co. Kerry, are composed of different rock types. Schists and quartzites probably more than 500 million years old are found throughout Donegal, Wicklow, and Mayo, while granites are seen in Connemara and the Mournes, sandstones in the central plain, limestone in the Burren, and chalk in Co. Antrim, where basaltic flows led to wonders like the Giant's Causeway. The hills are, of course, the most scenic areas of the country but the midlands, too often thought of as flat, rarely disappoint, coming up with interesting groups of undulating hills that add variety to the landscape. Common to lowlands and higher lands is turf or peat, the development of which can be spoken of in terms of only a few thousand years, in comparison to the millions of years of geologic time.

It is surprising to learn that the now treeless karst limestone "desert" of the Burren in north Clare was originally forested, and had its wood cut down as early as the Stone Age, leading to denudation and dispersal of the soil cover. It is equally unexpected to find that, until some twenty thousand years ago, almost the whole of Ireland —except for a narrow strip running along the south coast—was covered with glaciers of the last Ice Age. Their retreat has left their vestiges on the landscape in the form of scratchings on stones, the bumpy drumlins of Co. Cavan and, in half-submerged form, in Clew Bay in County Mayo. Also of glacial origin are the eskers, tall and narrow raised mounds weaving their way like snakes across the midland plains, where they are often used as roads today.

After the English cut down much of Ireland's remaining primeval forest to build their ships and deny the Irish rebels sylvan bolt-holes in the seventeenth century, the Irish landscape began to take on the appearance it has today. The hedges and walls that form such interesting irregular patterns in the countryside are largely the result of different ways of dividing up the land that came about in the last quarter of the second millennium. Distributing land among the children of a family, particularly common in the nineteenth century, meant very small fields and holdings ill-equipped to support a population that rose to eight million in 1841, but which famine and emigration halved to roughly its present level two years later.

The Mourne Mountains

The Kingdom of Mourne, as it is known, is a wonderful self-contained area of mountain in Co. Down that forms the south-eastern corner of the province of Ulster. Geologically one of the youngest parts of Ireland, its granite hills have "their heads in the clouds and their feet in the sea," in the words of E. Estyn Evans, one of their most ardent admirers and biographers, and, as the sister of another great geographer, Robert Lloyd Praeger, put it, here are "low hills and high hills sitting down together." The source of the Mourne mountains' varied character is the rock that forms them—granite, fired underground and slowly cooled to give a crystalline quality but also a rough, unyielding nature. Yet the gentle, hard-working folk of the Mournes have known how to mold it to their needs. The smaller stones, many left behind and even given a certain rounding as the Ice Age glaciers pounded and left them for dead in the fields, were used by the people to build thick-set stone walls, one of which—three feet wide and twenty miles long—climbs and falls from peak to peak fencing off the catchment area of the Silent Valley reservoir. Other outcrops they exploited commercially in quarries, and what W.R. Rodgers described as "the tiny clustered clinks of little chisels tinkling tirelessly on stone" provided Belfast and Lancashire with stones to curb and pave the streets. Estyn Evans tells of the stonemasons of Annalong, a fishing port in the Mournes, who used to spend the spring in New York fixing the sidewalks after the preceding winter's damage, while others, it was said, crossed the Atlantic just to see what time it was on the other side.

ABOVE AND OPPOSITE: There is a certain magnificence about the Mournes, their irregular silhouette of peaks forming an impressive scenic backdrop whether viewed from Belfast or Dublin, between which they lie. It is not unusual for the summits to rise to over two thousand feet, and Slieve Donard is their monarch *(Slieve* or *Sliabh* being the Gaelic for "mountain"). Donard was a pagan who, true to the conservative and traditional nature of mountain men, took a long time to change over to Christianity, and then only after St. Patrick had used all the superior powers of persuasion to convince him. He later retired to a cell on top of the mountain where local legend says that he still says Mass every Sunday, and where people come to venerate him on an annual pilgrimage. But locals also revere Slieve Binnion, where Boirche, the first king of Mourne, tended his cows and kept watch on happenings in the valley below.

PAGES 66-67: To some, blue may seem a cold color, but in nature's realm it can dance with the joy of a Glockenspiel ("the play of a bell" in German) when the bluebells come out in spring. Usually best under trees and shrubs, they proliferate in open country among the Wicklow Hills, as here near Sally Gap, where they contrast with the fresh yellow of the gorse (called "whins" in Northern Ireland).

ABOVE: The blue of the sky and the bluish tinge of the hills mix their palettes enchantingly in the hills of Connemara, with some of the Twelve Pins or Bens as seen from Ballynahinch.

LEFT: The evening sun, too, can bring out strange effects in color in the West of Ireland, where the blue of the sky is reflected in Doo Lough in the Mweelrea mountains of Mayo. Fifty years ago and more, the painter Paul Henry used the wonderful clouds among the western hills of Connacht to create his own landscape image of Ireland that captivated his own and later generations. But some other painters must find Ireland annoyingly capricious, since the colors can change so rapidly before they can be recorded on canvas—but of such is the charm of Ireland.

Other than the fish, what is it that draws fishermen to seek the waters of the wild? Is it the peace engendered by lake waves mildly lapping, the gentle motion of a cradle as the boat sways side to side, or just escape from humdrum to nature's bounteous ride? On the calm Lakes of Killarney *(right)*, the silence all can hear, but on another, Lough Ree in Westmeath *(above)*, the sound of the wind among the rushes at the parting of the day brings dissipation of the storm clouds and contentment in its way.

OVERLEAF (PAGE 72): Of the five fingers that stretch out into the Atlantic Ocean from the southwestern rim of Ireland, the northern-most—and perhaps most fascinating of all—is the Dingle Peninsula. It gets its name from a medieval town close to its western extremity, near which its coastline is the debris of a vast volcanic explosion many millions of years ago. This event created the rugged outline on bays like Clogher *(pages 72–74)* and beaches such as Coumeenole *(pages 76–77)*. Clogher Bay looks westward at a group of offshore islands including Inishtooskert ("the northern island"), not inhabited for a century, and the neighboring Blasket Islands to the south, abandoned less than fifty years ago after having given birth to a prolific and gifted school of writers in Irish.

The highest mountain on the Dingle Peninsula is Mount Brandon (3027 feet) and, for centuries, it was a place of pilgrimage held annually in honor of St. Brendan. His epithet was "the Navigator," because one of Europe's best-known medieval travelogues, the *Navigatio Brendani,* told of how this sixth-century saint hopped from one island to another, starting from the Dingle Peninsula and landing probably on the Faroes, Iceland, and Greenland before possibly reaching the North American continent. The boat he and his twelve disciples used was a currach, a craft made of a light wooden frame covered with leather (replaced by canvas on its modern counterpart), which glides as if miraculously on top of the waves. Such vessels are stored upside down on blocks, and are carried by men who get underneath and raise them up on their shoulders to be brought to the water's edge for launching *(above).* Throughout the Dingle Peninsula, such a vessel is aptly called a *naomhóg*—literally, "a beetle"—after their multi-legged, insect-like appearance as they are carried to the shore.

PAGES 76-77: The beach at Coumeenole, on the Dingle Peninsula.

PAGES 78-79: A gathering of gannets on the Saltee Islands off the Wexford coast.

The coast of Co. Antrim is the only place in Ireland where chalk outcrops are found, creating steep white cliffs that are reflected in the local place-names—Larrybane *(left)*, *(bane* means "white" in Gaelic), and The White Rocks *(above)*.

81

Ireland's only World Heritage site is the Giant's Causeway on the Co. Antrim coast, an accolade justly earned because it is one of nature's truly great wonders. It is a honeycomb of thousands of columns with between three and nine sides that came into being when basalt flows began to cool into these curious shapes some sixty million years ago. Legend holds that it was built by the great folk hero Fionn MacCumhail (or Finn McCool), his name also associated with the other striking occurrence of this phenomenon—the Hebridean island of Staffa, where Fingal's Cave provided the title and the inspiration for Mendelssohn's famous overture.

Geologically impressive in a different way are the Cliffs of Moher on the Atlantic face of Co. Clare, where they rise to a height of almost seven hundred feet and create a series of headlands receding one behind the other along an eight-mile stretch of coast. Limestone forms the base for the superimposed flat beds of sandstone and shale above, the former recognizable through the tortuous worm casts of the Liscannor flags used on many an Irish floor, both inside and out. Here, too, legend has played its role in the (apocryphal) stories told about Máire Rua, Red Mary O'Brien of Leamaneagh. She was sought after by so many suitors that she sent each one off on a bronco-like exercise to tame a horse which suddenly sped away and brought each rider out across the Cliffs of Moher, there to be thrown off into the Atlantic waves below.

PAGES 84-85: Glenmacnass Waterfall in Co. Wicklow.

ABOVE: The Atlantic winds hit the west coast of Ireland at a rattling pace, bundling up the clouds and bringing the rainfall that makes Ireland green. Trees often lean to leeward in their wake, dying if exposed too long, and many people in the West of Ireland create a thick windbreak of trees to protect themselves and their houses.

RIGHT: Shelter belts of trees are found in the clean and ennobling landscape at the foot of Benbulben —known to many as the burial place of the poet, W.B. Yeats—which make an unforgettable impression in their own right in the Co. Sligo countryside. The table mountain is formed of beds of carboniferous limestone and, in time, the denudation of the rock caused boulders to fall down and make a ramp-like scree at the foot of the hill. The plateau on top still preserves some arctic flora which probably survives from the tundra vegetation that grew shortly after the ice caps retreated from the area some twenty thousand years ago.

OPPOSITE: One of the most beautiful places in southwest Ireland is Glengarriff, in Co. Cork, where a mild climate allows the luxuriant growth of flora and trees.

PAGES 88-89: Stone walls are a characteristic feature of many Irish landscapes, particularly in the limestone and granite areas where the nature of the stone can lend itself to wall building. Some of the walls—such as that creeping slowly, like a snake across the fields, to the banks of Lough Corrib in Co. Galway—are a foot or more thick, and these often served the dual purpose of clearing rocky fields and providing much needed labor.

RIGHT: Colorful flowers carpet the rocky landscape in the High Mournes, Co. Down.

BELOW: In addition to the thick walls, there are also smaller, thinner walls which—given the ubiquity of the building material—were a cheap and effective way of creating new field boundaries when land was being divided up among members of a family. The thinner the wall, the more difficult it was to build because, as in a house of cards, each stone had to balance on the one beneath it without the whole lot crashing down, particularly when someone climbed over it. Building such walls is a dying art since they are gradually being replaced by cement and chain-link fencing which have none of the charm, and will never get the patina, of an old-fashioned stone wall. The narrow walls have holes between the stones, so as to allow the wind to blow through, rather than knocking it down, which it could do if the wall were solid.

OPPOSITE: Each stone wall is different, each has its own character. In them the history of a landscape could be read, if we could but hear the story of their makers. The stone walls in the Black Valley in Co. Kerry were probably erected in the last century by the few inhabitants of this lonely place. They presumably left the county and the country to find company and work, leaving behind an empty cottage—one of thousands in the Irish countryside that are often associated with the sad tales of the Famine or emigration, or both.

From time immemorial, cattle have been the backbone of Irish society and its economy. Archaeological sites of the Stone Age have, when excavated, produced the bones of cattle that were obviously used for both their meat and their milk. One ferocious bull—or, to be more precise, two ferocious bulls—were the inspiration for the greatest saga of medieval Ireland. One night, when Queen Maeve of Connacht was comparing her property to that of her husband Ailill, she discovered to her chagrin that there was only one item he had which she did not have—a large brown bull. Since there was only one other beast of similar quality in the whole country, she determined she was going to get it—and assembled an army to march across Ireland to capture it in Co. Louth. But she had one mighty enemy in Cú Chulainn, the youthful hero at the court of King Conor Mac Nessa in Ulster, who took on and defeated the soldiers of her army one by one. However, she finally succeeded in snatching the bull at Cooley in Co. Louth (hence the name of the epic—*Táin Bó Cuailnge*—"*the Cattle Raid of Cooley*") and bringing it back home to Connacht where she could match it against Ailill's. The whole tale concludes in something of an anticlimax, however, when the two bulls charge at one another, and end up by leaving each other dead upon the field.

In comparison, the humble sheep has been keeping Ireland warm with its wool for more generations than one cares to remember. But any motorist will find it hard to forget the Irish sheep he meets on a narrow road in the middle of their five o'clock rush *(opposite)*, when they are often accompanied by a well-trained sheepdog herding its flock to the safety of a gated field. And when not on duty with the sheep, the dog sits outside his master's house on the roadside, waiting to pounce on any unsuspecting motorist who should dare to speed past without stopping to shake his paw. Sheep, however, have voracious appetites and are—regrettably—getting a bad reputation for causing erosion through over grazing, particularly on the hill slopes of the West of Ireland.

ABOVE: It is a little-known fact that peat bogs, like this one in Co. Kerry, cover one-sixth of the land of Ireland, giving the area they cover a treeless brown color only rarely interrupted by human habitation. It is formed when plants that do not rot in poorly drained land pile up on one another over the years, thus creating deposits that can reach a thickness of thirty feet or more. In places like the Céide Fields on the north coast of Mayo, prehistoric houses and stone walls dating from about four thousand years ago have been found underneath the peat, showing that, indeed, it is of fairly recent growth, and still growing at the rate of almost a foot per century.

The State has been exploiting turf for economic reasons—as a valuable substitute for expensive imported coal and oil—since 1934, its present semi-State body for the purpose, founded in 1946, called Bord na Móna ("The Turf Board"). The word *Móna,* meaning "turf," occurs in many Irish place-names. But the rural population of Ireland have been exploiting turf for themselves for many hundreds of years, particularly where wood was not available to keep the home fires burning in the depths of winter. If a family does not possess its own particular bog, it can rent a section and take out annually the amount it needs to keep the house warm.

Whether using a fork or *sleán* (pronounced "shlaun"), designed specifically for the purpose, a clean "spit" of peat is cut the depth of the tool, a process that can be repeated as the bog is cut down deeper and deeper, clearly leaving the mark of the implement on the clean-cut side of the bog-face. The turf is thrown up to the top of the bank, and then placed in neat "stooks," to dry for as long as it needs. Then, before the onset of winter, tractors or donkeys with creels (wickerwork panniers) bring home the turf from the bog for stacking in large—and often artistically built—piles beside the house. Many of the cottages of Connemara, like the one opposite, keep themselves warm under the thatch because of the turf heaped up beside it during the winter.

The Burren, an area of north Clare, boasts of having Ireland's most extraordinary landscape, the finest bare limestone plateau of its kind anywhere in northern Europe. Poet John Betjeman describes the evocative landscape as "Little fields with boulders dotted/Grey-stone shoulders saffron-spotted." The Burren is the remains of sea-bed limestone, fossil-rich, formed hundreds of millions of years ago, which lost its later covering of shale and sandstone to leave it the flat, dry, wrinkled landscape it is today. The dreaded Oliver Cromwell is said to have described the Burren as a place where there was "not enough wood to hang a man, not enough water to drown a man, and not enough earth to bury a man." But Cromwell did not get it even half right, for the Burren is far richer than he ever imagined.

Where the points of weakness in the stone created joints or cracks, and became widened through weathering, water percolated, and small pieces of earth gathered to give not only a growth of grass that provides wonderful winter grazing for cattle, but also a rich and varied flora, which, if uprooted (which it should never be!), would wither and die in any other conditions. Here is gathered an inexplicable combination of arctic and alpine plants that would not normally grow together elsewhere, and whose very presence here continues to puzzle botanists. Unusual orchids, rare plants such as mountain avens (*Dryas octopetala*), the rock rose (*Helianthemum canum*) and burnet rose (*Rosa pimpinellifolia*, top left), bloody cranesbill (*Geranium sanguineum*), thrift (*Armeria maritima*), and, as the Burren's logo, the gentian (*Gentiana verna*), can be found in the rock joints, known as grykes, which can create the most unexpected sculptural forms in the greyish-blue limestone.

OPPOSITE: The sun sets in the quiet county of Fermanagh, where visitors come to fish for the plentiful perch, trout, and salmon that stock the region's tranquil, reedy lakes.

ABOVE, LEFT AND RIGHT, OPPOSITE: Snow is a comparatively rare visitor to most of Ireland, though when it does fall, the country comes to a standstill, unaccustomed as it is to such conditions. Snow does, however, fall first and fastest in Northern Ireland, where it creates problems for the farmers in keeping their sheep alive and fed.

PAGE 102: Nature sinks to rest after the sun casts its evening glow from beneath the horizon over the still waters of Lough Neagh in Northern Ireland, the country's largest lake.

Things can have been little different a thousand years ago, when an old Irish poet—anonymous as usual—used short staccato images to conjure up the year's darkest season, given here in Kuno Mayer 's translation:

My tidings for you:—the stag bells
Winter snows, summer is gone.

Wind high and cold, low the sun,
Short his course, sea running high.

Deep-red the bracken, shapes are hidden,
The wild-goose has raised his wonted cry.

Cold has caught the wings of birds:
Season of ice—these are my tidings.

V IRISH GARDENS

The garden where the praties grow" was the title of a well-known song by Johnny Paterson (1840–1889), and it reminds us that, for many Irish who lived in the last century, a garden was a patch where you grew your life-supporting potatoes and precious little else. But, for those who had the mind and means to do so, there were also more purely ornamental flower, shrub, and tree gardens, which had been created and nurtured in the country since the seventeenth century. Few of these early examples survive—for gardens can be ephemeral if they do not have tender loving care constantly lavished upon them. Yet there is still a considerable number of gardens that have been in existence for well over a century, and one of the most encouraging aspects of Ireland's fragile floral heritage is the number of wonderful gardens that have been developed during the last twenty-five or thirty years, four of which—Butterstream, Lakemount, Ardcarraig, and Helen Dillon's in Dublin—are featured in the pages that follow.

But none of these would have come into existence without the help of the unique Irish climate, which makes the country such an ideal environment for gardening. Ireland is at the same latitude north of the equator as New-foundland and Hudson Bay, yet it rarely ever gets their frost or snow. Instead, it basks in the warmth of the Gulf Stream, which keeps the temperatures up in winter—the January average is 5 degrees C, 41 degrees Fahrenheit—and mild in summer, when the July mean is around 15 degrees C, or just under 60 degrees Fahrenheit. As far back as the eighth century, the Venerable Bede, an English historian, praised Ireland's mild and healthy climate, and, a hundred years later, an Irishman in exile, Donatus of Fiesole, envisaged his country from afar as being "benign to the body, in air and mellow soil" (in the words of Liam de Paor's translation from the Latin). It is the combination of this mild climate, the constant moisture in the air, the varying landscape, and the different soils which make Ireland into what Charles Nelson has described as "one of the great gardening lands." To this, Helen Dillon would add the low light (because of its northerly location on the globe), which can bring astonishing moments even on a dull and misty day, and it is surely those few seconds when everything is right that can make a paradise on earth.

Furthermore, Helen Dillon would maintain that even in her small suburban Garden of Eden she can grow more plant varieties than anywhere else in the northern hemisphere, but they behave in a peculiarly Irish way because of the rain and the constant moisture in the air. No matter how she—and others—try to impose order and organization on a garden, plants will step in and take over, and do things their own way—not hers or theirs. It is perhaps not surprising that the man who turned formal gardening on its head in the last century was an Irishman named William Robinson, the title of whose book *The Wild Garden* (1870) so neatly sums up the "romantic jungle" atmosphere Irish gardeners can hope to achieve voluntarily or otherwise. Formal features and artificial effects are thus not always appropriate in an Irish setting, and nature certainly tends to reign supreme in Irish gardens, and plays hospitable host to many a foreign plant. Trees, shrubs, and flowers introduced from exotic climes in the last century adapted themselves superbly to the Irish soil and climate, and often grew taller than those in their homeland, as Mount Stewart, for instance, can show so superbly.

The different soils and landscape backgrounds, as well as natural features such as rivers and streams (Butterstream, for example), have helped to mold Irish gardens into the magnetic attractions they are. It is the bounty of nature in its mildness and moisture, and the way that talented and imaginative Irish gardeners have used their skill to foster the planting of an extraordinarily wide range of species, that makes Irish gardens so very different, and such a joy to behold and wander through, whether public or private.

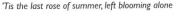

'Tis the last rose of summer, left blooming alone

All her lovely companions are faded and gone.

Thomas Moore's lovely ballad automatically comes to mind on entering the National Botanic Gardens in the Dublin suburb of Glasnevin, for there is a cultivar of the rose that is said to have inspired the poet's melancholy musings. The Gardens were founded in 1795 on already fruitful ground, for some of the yews still standing go back to the 1740s when the famous essayist Joseph Addison is said to have sought inspiration as he walked among them. In the 1840s orchid seeds were germinated here for the first time in garden surroundings, and seedlings grown to the flowering stage. The director at the time was David Moore and, though he was one of the few to realize at the time that the potato blight that caused the Great Famine of 1845–1847 was due to fungal disease, he narrowly missed discovering a treatment to stop the fungus in its deadly tracks. Had he succeeded, how different the world would be today!

To go to the Botanical Gardens is to enter a world of wonder away from the hustle and bustle of city life. The walks laid out in the last century bring one through a very selective collection of trees both rare and beautiful—species of oak, cypress, and cedar—of which the weeping Atlantic cedar must be regarded as the showpiece, together with the Chinese dove (or handkerchief) tree (Davidia involucrata). Another fine specimen, however, is the stone pine (Pinus pinea), which dominates the rock garden (bottom right) that rises to a gentle pyramid with a cordyline, a plant from the southern hemisphere that has become very popular in Ireland because its resemblance to a genuine palm tree gives anyone's garden a distinctly subtropical appearance.

The Botanic Gardens have plenty to offer the plant lover. For the contemplative type, the rose garden (opposite) offers a considerable variety laid out in a formal and well-cared-for manner. For those who enjoy color to raise their spirits, early summer produces a glorious flood of blossoms of wondrous hues all over the gardens (top right), when red phlox and blue delphiniums hobnob with one another as chrysanthemums bask in their own reflected glory. In the background is seen the top of the Great Palm House, built in 1884. One of the most overpowering sensations of the Gardens, it has a steamy jungle-like atmosphere, with palms, bananas, creepers, and other exotica, where only Tarzan's cry is missing. Equally impressive as a piece of mid-Victorian glass-house engineering, with curved iron and panes of glass, is the Curvolinear Range, built by Richard Turner, who also constructed the glass-houses at Kew Gardens in London.

As a teacher of the next generation of gardeners, a propagating center for rare plants to help their survival, as a reference collection of more than national significance, and a recreation for native and visitor alike, the National Botanic Gardens plays a key role in continuing the excellence of Irish gardens.

The gardens at Mount Stewart, on the shores of Strangford Lough in Co. Down, are one of the most striking and idiosyncratic gardens in the whole of Ireland, now magnificently maintained by the National Trust. At its center is the house built in two stages during the latter half of the eighteenth century and during the first half of the nineteenth, and it was its neoclassical appearance that dictated the formal layout of the surrounding gardens when their presiding genius, Edith, Lady Londonderry, came to live here in 1921. She was fortunate in having had mature conifers and an artificial lake of the 1830s and 1840s to provide her with a backdrop, and it was she who planted and designed much of the eighty acres of gardens, which are such a delight to walk through as her ideas have now reached such a bountiful maturity. She prided herself rightly on having "discovered" that the estate had just the right climate for planting—subtropical, with help from the Gulf Stream, thirty-five inches of rainfall annually, and a lime-free soil. From her sitting room, she could look out over one of her masterpieces, the square sunken garden *(opposite)* where the central lawn is framed by formal low hedges in curvaceous

sweeps containing a wild profusion of yellow, blue, and purple flowers. An initial sketch suggesting a layout, drafted by the English landscape architect Gertrude Jekyll is, incidentally, preserved in the library of the University of California at Berkeley. A break in the stone and timber pergola surrounding three of its sides gives a view through to the shamrock garden, its three leaves created by a yew hedge. Near its center is the Red Hand of the province of Ulster, created with seasonally planted begonias, and towering above it is an Irish harp, meticulously shaped in topiary.

Down near the stream entering the lake *(above, left)*, Lady Londonderry planted groups of flowering trees and shrubs including *Acer palmatum,* pampas grass, and *Kniphofia* (better known as red-hot pokers). But she also had time for a wonderful piece of drollery, the Dodo Terrace *(above, right)*. She created a loggia filled with birds and animals—some real, some imaginary—such as the dinosaur illustrated here, carved by a local stonemason named Beattie. The animals gave their names to members of the Ark Club that she had founded in her London house in 1915, and which included many famous people among the politicians, soldiers, painters, and sculptors of the day.

Birr Castle, ancestral home of the Earl and Countess of Rosse, was built over an earlier castle in the 1620s, and has undergone many advantageous changes since, making it into one of Ireland's most comfortable stately homes. Brendan, the seventh earl, certainly has gardening in the family. His ancestors have been planting here for three hundred years, both of his parents were gardeners, and he continues an old family tradition in still supporting plant-collecting expeditions to the Orient. Birr has many claims to fame, one being the recently restored telescope (through which spiral nebulae were first discovered), and the garden is another. The planted area extends over 180 acres, and one of the garden's outstanding characteristics is the collection of oriental plants, which have grown very well in this midland location, where there is less rainfall and sharper winter frosts than nearer the coast. Down by the lakeside *(opposite, left)*, normally acid-loving rhododendrons seem to thrive surprisingly well on alkaline soil, keeping company with the skunk cabbage *(lysichiton)*. More edible cabbages can be seen in the kitchen garden *(opposite, right)*, where they add their own particular quality to the autumn light, with a rich growth of trees offering them suitable protection from the wind. But perhaps Birr's horticultural *pièce de résistance* is the horn-beam allee *(right)*, its falling leaves adding their ground color to the mellowing trellised branches above, all leading the eye to a classical statue in the background, as if seen through the riotously decorated nave of a rococo church.

"The approach to Cork by Glanmire is magnificent; a sort of sea avenue up to the town, with beautiful banks on each side, studded over with tasteful villas." Those are the comments of the poet Thomas Moore as he passed through the village of Glanmire on the outskirts of Cork in 1823, and they act as an introduction to the lyricism of Lakemount, the garden that Brian Cross and his mother developed over the last few decades on what had once been a chicken farm on the crown of Barnavara hill at Glanmire. With rich, acid soil on a south-facing slope overlooking Cork Harbor, the garden (open by appointment) has flourished despite exposure to winds, and is informally divided up into various areas covering a two-acre site. The main view is over a lawn *(above)*, which is bordered by a huge variety of plants, including a *Lobelia tupa* in the foreground. *Lush* is the only word to describe the plants around the lily pond *(opposite)*, with a striking *Carex* grass on the left and three *Phormium* overlooking the pool.

But even more stunning is the pendulous *Acer (right)*, which adds such brilliance to the autumn color. Being an art teacher with the added advantage of having very green fingers, it is no wonder that Brian Cross has been three times overall winner of the Irish Tourist Board/National Gardens Association Competition.

Butterstream—what a lovely name—is a garden on the outskirts of the town of Trim in Co. Meath created by Jim Reynolds, a local farmer's son. When little more than a child, his father allowed him to plant roses in a corner of a field he could call his own, but, like most teenagers, he sought out little that would over-tax his energies. In his twenties, however, he extended his vision when he visited larger gardens in Ireland and Britain, Sissinghurst in Kent impressing him particularly because it was not dominated by a well-kept Georgian mansion and was just a garden sitting in the countryside. That is precisely what he himself has made of Butterstream, and perhaps also what attracted Prince Charles when he made Butterstream his only garden stop during his visit to Ireland in 1995. It also appealed to *The Good Gardener's Guide,* which awarded him its highest, two-star accolade for all his solitary efforts.

The garden is a delightful mixture of the formal and the natural. Beside a beautifully mown croquet lawn, enclosed by conifers interrupted by a playful classical portico and a fine summer house containing the mallets and balls for the game, is a gentle profusion of potted plants oozing out onto the grass. One of these *(right, top)* is *Fuchsia magellanica versicolor,* with leaves of a different and lighter green from that found growing wild in the lanes of Co. Kerry, and beside it is a youthful boxwood from the Azores—the largest-leaved variety of its kind. By autumn, the hydrangea next to it is ready to shed its petals. In contrast, the herbaceous border *(right, bottom)* is a riot of color in July, dominated by the mauve-blue *Campanula lactiflora* in the center, with the phlox on the left playing a minor role as it luxuriates beneath the white willow herb. On the right, the race to outgrow the rest was won by the yellow *Thalictrum speciosissimum,* but even the lovely day lily in the bottom center gets plenty of light to keep it smiling.

Butterstream is full of delightful surprises. Like a Moorish palace, every corner turned produces the unexpected—a formal box-hedged compartment, a cul-de-sac, or a wonderful pool garden with a classical stone portico reflected among the water lilies.

 On a sunny day, the blended colors impress as they recede one behind the other, until an enclosing hedge blocks their further expansion *(above, left)*. The texture of the herbaceous border appeals to the eye, as the campanula mingles with thalictrum in the upper echelons, while below a catmint *(Nepeta govaniana)* and blue phlox clamber for space at their feet. Turning a gentle corner beyond the border brings the visitor face to face with the head of a terracotta Medusa *(above, right)*. But don't be afraid! Being more a jocose jester's mask, it is harmless fun—and beckons to further exploration in this Aladdin's garden.

Beaulieu, close to the northern bank of the Boyne estuary not far from Drogheda, has been handed down from one generation to the next within the same family since the house was first built in the 1660s. It is above all the women of the family who have been putting their stamp on the garden (open on summer mornings), and none more so than the present owner, Mrs. Nesbit Waddington, who has been continuing the matriarchal pattern by passing on to her daughter her own great enthusiasm for gardening.

Although the fine house would have been the obvious focal point for the garden, the main development has been in the Kitchen Garden, with the tower of the family church, built in 1807, as the point of orientation *(top left, and right)*. Though scarcely more than a foot high, the box hedges come out strongly as the lines that create the ground-plan, and they subdivide the gardens into compartments. It is the contents of these hedged-in areas that create the color, whether it be old-fashioned roses, sweet williams *(right)*, snapdragons, and wall-flowers *(far right)*, or forget-me-nots *(bottom)*. A Mediterranean charm is evoked by the lavender under the old apple tree *(opposite)*. The garden slopes gently, but the eye is often led up or down towards a building that closes off the vista. This may be the church tower, reminding one to think of the creator of those lovely flowers, or the rustic wooden Victorian garden house, which, in summer (as here), seeks shelter in the shadow of a yew.

116

"The finest suburban garden in Britain or Ireland" is how Helen Dillon's garden at 45 Sandford Road in Dublin has been described, and it would not be presumptuous to add "or probably anywhere else in Europe for that matter." This garden, only half an hour's walk from the center of Dublin, should only be spoken about in hushed superlatives. Less than an acre in extent, it manages to display a wonderful variety of plants that Helen is constantly reevaluating for their position, their color, and their contribution to the overall effect. She is a plantswoman *par excellence* who, nevertheless, does not let her collector's instinct get in the way of a proper sense of order, quality, and appropriateness. Informality in a formally planned garden is her secret, though, to keep the eye constantly alert, she makes her straight lines purposely crooked.

Her flower borders have well-planned matching colors, the dwarf yellow *Verbascum* "Frosted Gold" in the foreground *(left)* luxuriating with many others beneath the towering presence of the golden variety of the Irish yew *Taxus baccata "Fastigiata Aurea."* Looking out from her 1830s terraced housed over the back garden, the view *(above)* looks out on a pair of sphinxes guarding the entrance to the bordered lawn manicured twice weekly to perfection by Helen's supportive husband, Val. Beyond that are the indescribably rich colors of the plants that the Irish public knows so well not only from its visits to the gardens but also from their frequent appearance on her very popular television series, and her many lecture tours across the globe.

A pocket of hazel scrub surviving from generations past was the unpromising start to the challenge facing Lorna MacMahon in her quest to provide an interesting garden surrounding her home at Ardcarraig, just outside Galway city. Thin acid soil, poor in nutrients, did not make her task any easier, but within a quarter of a century she has succeeded in making one of the most unusual gardens in the West of Ireland. The hazel has now been tamed and a path from the house leads through the woodland to a series of undulating compartments that have been wrested from a wilderness and created into very differing entities. One of the most exotic of these is the Japanese garden (above), where she diverted a stream to create a pool exuding the peace that is symbolized by the Yukumi dora, a two-hundred-year-old stone snow lantern of a kind found in sacred Japanese gardens and here given verisimilitude with the creation of a miniature Mount Fuji.

Mrs. MacMahon was also able to utilize the advantages of a sunken hollow in front of her house, and there she outwitted the harsh Atlantic winds by initiating the planting with low-growing shrubs, as well as dwarf conifers such as the golden weeping cedar and the upright golden yew, which have now grown beyond all expectations. Near the rear of the house, she built a sunken Mediterranean-style garden (right), enlivened by a modern version of an ancient Cretan beehive pot, still made in Crete in the old traditional manner.

VI TOWNS AND CITIES

Dublin is Ireland's largest city, and the population living around the shores of Dublin Bay and its hinterland amounts to well over one million people—between a quarter and a third of the population of the whole island. Dublin is bursting at the seams, and this helps us to appreciate the foresight of the Norse Vikings in choosing this advantageous and expansive location for their first major urban trading center in 841. Before their arrival, the monasteries were the nearest the Irish had come to creating towns, and it was the Vikings who were also responsible for a number of other Irish towns around the coast, some of which—such as Wexford and Waterford—still contain Scandinavian elements in their names. These Vikings came temporarily to trade, and stayed to settle. Dublin was one of their most important settlements outside their homeland, and this favored status came about because Dublin was well-placed to act as a trading station halfway along the Viking sea routes up and down the Atlantic coast of Europe. Within Ireland, Dublin came in time to be a political pawn, a prize worth fighting for, and its crucial position in the country was grasped when the Normans occupied it shortly after their arrival in 1169/70. It was to remain the center of an occupying power until 1922, and it is since then that its population has grown so enormously, causing a corresponding depopulation in other, particularly western, parts of the country. Dublin's earlier zenith was achieved between 1782 and 1800, when it was the center of an independent Irish parliament, after which its international importance declined.

But, throughout Ireland, the nineteenth century saw the rise of a prosperous new middle class, who were the backbone of the development of so many Irish towns. Some of these urban centers had existed already in the Middle Ages, but others developed from just a few small dwellings into prosperous market towns, characterized by a solid bank or two, and two-storey houses, often with a shop on the ground floor and the family living in comfort "above the shop" on the first floor. Further down the scale were the villages, even today a happy mix of single- and two-storey houses, with the current economic boom bringing with it the ribbon development of bungalows along the roads that lead out of Ireland's villages and towns.

Maritime commerce ensured that Ireland's largest towns were on the coast—Dublin, Belfast, Cork, Waterford, Galway, and Wexford, for instance—but many also flourished inland, particularly where there is rich land in the surrounding countryside. No matter how small the settlement, there is nearly always at least one pub in the village, which can act as a social meeting place for the local farming community. Even villages can often boast of having two churches, the increasing confidence of the Catholic population in the nineteenth century being reflected in their having the taller spire.

ABOVE: By a curious quirk of history, Dublin has two cathedrals, neither in the hands of the Catholic majority, but both lovingly cared for by the small Church of Ireland (Anglican) community in the city. St. Patrick's is the younger of the two, dating from the thirteenth century, and gets its name because tradition said that the national apostle baptized Dubliners at a well here some fifteen hundred years ago. Having been allowed to fall into a state of considerable disrepair, the cathedral was restored to its former harmonious glory through generous contributions by the Guinness family in the last century, an act of philanthropy that its most famous dean, Jonathan Swift, would have most heartily applauded.

OPPOSITE: The river Liffey flows through the center of Dublin city, and divides it neatly into the north and south sides, which have always had a friendly rivalry with one another. But the two parts are happily linked by a series of bridges that can clearly be made out in the lights of Dublin's nightlife.

ABOVE: The year 1977 saw the launch of U2, an Irish Rock band once described as "the biggest in the universe bar none!" Its charismatic character, as well as the political and religious undertones in its lyrics, gave it an aura very different from the rest, and when *The Joshua Tree* was released in 1987, the world began to speak of U2 more as a phenomenon than a band. The recording studio was in Windmill Lane down near the Dublin docks, and its exterior wall became almost a cult object among the band's passionate army of followers, who covered the whole surface with a colorful collection of graffiti.

OPPOSITE: Dublin is famous for its classical architecture, commonly known as Georgian because it was created during the reign of the first four Georges, kings of England and, more particularly, in the time of George III (1760–1820). Its red-brick houses reflect the elegance of the period, and they are best known for their well-proportioned doorways in the area of, and between, Merrion Square and Fitzwilliam Square on the south side of the Liffey. Each differs in design *(top)*, but common to almost all of them are the door frame with pillar and Doric or Ionic column on each side, sometimes a side-window on either flank, and nearly always with a graceful fan-light in the semicircular tympanum above the door.

Not many Georgian house interiors are open to the public, but guests of the Merrion Hotel in Upper Merrion Street are able to enjoy the superb craftsmanship of the wooden doors carved in the taste of the time, with floral motifs proliferating among the entablature of its classical doorways *(bottom, center and right)*.

Among Dublin's greatest public buildings of the period is the Custom House, built by the architect James Gandon in the years 1781–1791. Its detailing is of the highest caliber, and the architect had the good fortune to find an Irish sculptor, Edward Smyth, whose talents matched his requirements so well. It was Smyth who carved the heads over the Custom House arches, each representing an Irish river, such as the river Lagan illustrated here *(bottom, left)*. An earlier set of Irish bank notes bore a drawing of one or other of these heads, and the higher the value of the bank note, the greater was the smile of the head on it!

The city of Belfast, capital of Northern Ireland, has developed over the last four centuries from being a small market town dealing in cotton and linen to the thriving metropolis of over half a million inhabitants it is today. It is beautifully situated in the valley where the river Lagan flows into Belfast Lough, its center dominated by the imposing dome of City Hall (1902–1906), in front of which the citizens meet, protest, and celebrate the New Year with fireworks.

The nineteenth-century character of most of the city's remarkable architecture reflects its period of greatest affluence, which continued into our own century. In the past, the famous shipyards of Harland and Wolff often manufactured more tonnage than any others, their most famous product being the *Titanic*. Paneling intended for the interior of its sister ship, the *Britannic*, ended up in the first floor restaurant of one of Belfast's greatest gems, the Crown Bar Liquor Saloon on Great Victoria Street, with its beautiful tiled facade of 1898 *(opposite)* preserved by the National Trust.

RIGHT: You are never very far away from water in Ireland, and it plays an important role in the country's life. In the form of the sea surrounding the island, water provides the boating community with endless possibilities for enjoyment, as at Bullock Harbor on a corner of Dublin Bay, where fishermen find fun, and excursions can be made to Dalkey Island in the distance.

BELOW: Most of Ireland's larger towns are located directly on the sea and played an important role in long-distance overseas trade. Spain and Iceland were among the maritime partners of the western city of Galway, where Kenny's is a well-known mecca for book and art collectors alike.

OPPOSITE, TOP LEFT: With such an inexhaustible resource outside their front door, it is no wonder that many Irish towns face directly onto the sea, with only a roadway separating them from the quay, as at Kinvara on Galway Bay.

OPPOSITE, TOP RIGHT: The port of Cobh, from which so many Irish emigrants left for America, enjoys the protection of Cork Harbor, and passengers entering it on large liners today can enjoy the dramatic backdrop of the houses that cling in serried ranks to the sloping hillside.

OPPOSITE, BELOW: Water from the Liffey gives Guinness its own special flavor, and it, together with Murphy's and Beamish, provide the country with a stout that is the staple pint of many an Irishman, to be quaffed gently to the sounds of music, or just savored outside the pub at the end of a hard day's work in summer.

VII PEOPLE OF IRELAND

Ulster poet John Hewitt neatly sums up the amalgam that has gone into the making of the Irish people of today:

Kelt, Briton, Saxon, Dane, and Scot,
Time and this island tied a crazy knot.

The genes of many races flow in their veins, and there would be a general consensus that the mixture has turned out to be particularly successful. The freckles and occasional red hair of youth, together with the blue eyes and dark hair of the Irish colleens (from the Gaelic word *cailín,* "a girl") has become something of a stereotype, and not entirely without reason. It is, however, difficult to define a particularly Irish face, which does nevertheless stand out more in other countries than it does at home. In size, the Irish range from the small and dark to the tall and fair (in days gone by, you had to be six feet tall before you could join the Gardai, the Irish police force).

It is very difficult to get a rational and unbiased characterization of the Irish, though one thing is certain and that is that the buffoon image of the "stage Irishman" is both exaggerated and outdated. What you see in an Irish person is what you want to see—it depends on where you are coming from. You might think that the outsider would give you the most balanced view. But even that can be doubted from the assessment of one well-known English literary figure, Dr. Samuel Johnson, no great friend of Ireland, who averred that "the Irish are a fair people;—they never speak well of one another," though it should be said that the Irish on occasions would be prepared to describe themselves as being "a nation of begrudgers." In pleasant contrast, Johnson's fellow countryman, the Earl of Birkenhead, found the Irish to be "a people so individual in its genius, so tenacious in love or hate, so captivating in its nobler moods" and, in an address to the Irish people in 1812, the English romantic poet, Percy Bysshe Shelley, declared:

Oh, Ireland! thou emerald of the ocean, whose sons are generous and brave, whose daughters are honorable and frank and fair, thou art the isle on whose green shores I have desired to see the standard of liberty erected—a flag of fire—a beacon at which the world shall light the torch of freedom!

The average Irish person could well be described as being easy-going, courteous and affable, helpful and hospitable, more solicitous about other people's welfare than his or her own money, conservative, bibulous and good-humored, great raconteurs and philosophers with time to think and talk—though not necessarily in that order! They can be pleasantly inquisitive too, wanting to know where you come from and what you think of their country. What the Irish person certainly has is a wizardry with words, an unconscious eloquence that comes from using a wide vocabulary in an imaginative way, with plays on words commonplace (strikingly noticeable on the advertising billboards), punning a pardonable sin, and a love of the pithy phrase brought to a high art by its greatest practitioner, Oscar Wilde. The loom of language has led to a remarkable literature, some in Gaelic, but best known in English. Which nation on earth of Ireland's size could boast of four Nobel prize-winners in the field of literature—W.B. Yeats , G. B. Shaw, Samuel Beckett, and most recently, Seamus Heaney?

Old habits die hard, as the proverb says, and the hardest last longest of all. This surely applies to Ireland's oldest pilgrimage, which takes place every year to Croagh Patrick, Co. Mayo. When seen from afar, this cone-shaped mountain seems predestined from its very form to have been chosen as one of Ireland's most sacred places. In prehistoric times it was almost certainly the location of an annual harvest celebration in honor of Lug, the good god of the pagan Celts, when people from miles around would have come to climb the mountain and meet their friends and relatives from the other side, make matches, settle disputes, or do whatever was required. The Christian church was very diplomatic in transforming this old pagan festival into a Christian one, timing it to coincide in date with its pagan predecessor—the last Sunday in July. In due course, St. Patrick came to replace Lug as the focal figure of what had, by then, become a Christian pilgrimage. The legend tells how St. Patrick went to the top of "the Reek," as the mountain is locally known, and fasted there for forty days—in obvious imitation of the biblical Moses.

Every year on the last Sunday of July, people still come to Croagh Patrick to participate in the annual pilgrimage, be they young or old, cleric or lay, and they make their way up a stony path to the peak, 2510 feet above Clew Bay, stick in hand, like any medieval pilgrim. Until recent years, the mountain was climbed in bare feet and by candlelight at night, but now almost everyone does it during the day and spares others the sight of their muddy toes. Confessions are heard, and prayers and Mass are said at the top, where an oratory was built in the early years of this century near another (now ruined) built more than a thousand years earlier.

What is meant to be a penitential pilgrimage turns out, however, to be quite a jolly affair. People chatter away to one another, laugh and crack jokes—and it seems to have changed little from the festival in honor of the good god Lug almost two millennia ago. The outer appearances may have altered somewhat, but the spirit remains the same.

LEFT, TOP: A young girl's dream among the hyacinths—her future is brighter now as Ireland experiences an economic boom.

LEFT, MIDDLE: On the Aran Islands, a man is a dog's best friend, and he smiles as he takes a break from digging his potatoes.

LEFT, BOTTOM: You don't have to be a youthful model to enjoy showing off your colorful clothes.

ABOVE: Life may be hard on the aging joints, but who worries too much if you have a positive outlook, and a guarding angel to keep you company?

ABOVE, RIGHT: Highly skilled craftsmen create fine art, like this Waterford crystal.

ABOVE: Christmas carols sung by robed choristers in Dublin are part of the seasonal celebrations.

ABOVE, RIGHT: Musicians at the Cliffs of Moher demonstrate how Co. Clare is a hub of Irish traditional music and song.

ABOVE, FAR RIGHT: On Bloomsday, July 16th, every year, the literary world dresses up in Dublin to do honor to the century's greatest novel, James Joyce's *Ulysses*, which describes happenings in the life of Leopold Bloom and his friends on that fateful date in 1904.

BOTTOM, RIGHT: Traditional Irish dancing has long been popular on both sides of the Atlantic, with the young girls dressed up in those gorgeous costumes mothers and others have spent days and nights decorating with Celtic art motifs.

TOP, LEFT: Ireland's own national football game is known as Gaelic where, unlike soccer, the ball may be touched by hand. It is played worldwide, wherever there are sporting Irishmen.

TOP, MIDDLE: Tug of war is a popular sport at local annual fairs in Ireland.

TOP, RIGHT: The traditional currach, a timber-framed boat with canvas cover used for fishing and island transport, is now often fitted with an outboard motor.

ABOVE, LEFT: Horse racing—the sport of kings—has been practiced in Irish regal circles since history began.

ABOVE, MIDDLE: A-hunting we will go.

ABOVE: The Royal National Life Boat Institution of Ireland, and its heroic crews, ensure the maritime safety of this seagoing people.

LEFT: In Ireland the very high number of courses makes golf into a game with occasional birdies for rich and poor alike.